The Home Buyer's Guide

Edited by
Bill Adler, Jr.

A Fireside Book
Published by Simon & Schuster, Inc.
New York

A Fireside Book
Published by Simon & Schuster, Inc.
Simon & Schuster Building
Rockefeller Center
1230 Avenue of the Americas
New York, New York 10020

FIRESIDE and colophon are registered trademarks of
Simon & Schuster, Inc.

Designed by Irving Perkins Associates

Manufactured in the United States of America

Printed and bound by Fairfield Graphics

10   9   8   7

Library of Congress Cataloging in Publication Data

Adler, Bill
The home buyer's guide.

"A Fireside book."
1. House buying. 2. Mortgage loans. 3. Real estate
business. I. Title.
HD1379.A34   1984   643'.12   83-27134

ISBN: 0-671-50533-5

This book is intended to provide accurate, up-to-date information with regard to the subject matter covered. The Author and
the Publisher, however, do not guarantee complete freedom
from error.

Table of Contents

5

Foreword

The single most important purchase a person can make is a house. But deciding which house to buy can also be very frustrating and perplexing. Fluctuating mortgage rates, changing neighborhoods, a growing family, a plethora of available appliances, and variable workmanship all contribute to the great uncertainty many home buyers face.

The *Home Buyer's Guide* can alleviate many of the dilemmas encountered when searching for a house. It presents a clear, carefully organized approach to finding and securing a home that will be a pleasure for you and your children to live in. Developed from numerous United States government publications and studies on home buying, this guide is the most authoritative book ever published on how to buy a house.

Chapter 1 examines whether it is better to buy or to rent; it discusses how to explore investment conditions and apply them to your own financial situation. Chapter 2 presents a workable strategy for searching for a house. It discusses choosing the right neighborhood and the right house, using a real-estate broker, and how to know what the house will cost. Once you have found your dream home, paying for it becomes the next important step. Settlement costs and procedures are explained in Chapter 3. Chapter 4 provides a systematic approach to understanding mortgages. It tells you how to get the best possible mortgage and what to do if you cannot meet payments. Various strategies to creative financing are described here. Chapter 5 focuses on maintaining your home. Two invaluable appendices are included: a dictionary of housing terms and mortgage comparison charts.

I hope this book will help make your search for a new home easy—and a pleasure, as well.

Bill Adler, Jr.
Washington, D.C.

Chapter 1

Rent or Buy?

Should you rent or buy?

At some time in your life, you are likely to face a choice between owning or renting a house or other shelter. The decision to own or rent depends on many things. You can approach this decision by considering these three aspects:

- The personal-preference aspect: What kind of shelter meets your preferences and needs?
- The cost aspect: How much is it going to cost and how much can you spend each month for shelter?
- The investment aspect: How can you make the best investment of your money while obtaining shelter that meets your needs?

THE PERSONAL-PREFERENCE ASPECT. Looking at it from the first aspect, you will want to consider such factors as your age and family status, the stability of employment of the various members of the family, and the likelihood of your moving from one location to another.

Beyond these, the choice has some highly subjective elements. Do you like to "putter around" the house and yard on do-it-yourself projects, or do you dislike having to be responsible for maintenance, small repairs, lawn tending? Is the idea of "putting down roots" and gaining homeowner status in the community important to you?

Because shelter requirements and wants vary widely from individual to individual, from family to family, and

9

from one time to another, it is not possible to make any blanket statement about the kind of shelter that is "best." It is not likely that anyone else can give you much guidance about the weight to be given to all the different subjective considerations that enter into the decision.

THE COST ASPECT. A second aspect of the shelter decision concerns the costs you will incur and how much you can afford to spend for the kind of shelter you want and need. How different are costs of ownership and rental? Is there any way to compare them? What can you afford to spend? The amount you spend for shelter is influenced by personal considerations and by your income, both your present income and what you expect it to be in the future.

THE INVESTMENT ASPECT. The third aspect of shelter decisions concerns the prudent investment of your money. Would you be better off investing your money in home ownership over a period of time, or saving your down payment money and setting aside an amount each month, putting these funds into savings accounts or stocks and bonds, and so on?

This chapter helps you analyze these investment factors and apply them to your own situation, so that you can make a judicious decision as to the better course for you to follow. It describes and illustrates a technique for estimating the various costs and returns of being a homeowner or renter and then takes you step by step through the decision process so you can determine what the alternatives are for you, on the basis of choices and market conditions in your own area.

Can you afford to own?

If you are thinking of buying a home, you will need enough money to make a down payment on the purchase. This can be an important barrier to home ownership for families and individuals who do not have adequate savings. On the other hand, when savings are sufficient to allow a choice between buying or renting, there is a need to weigh the advantages of investing savings in shelter compared with other investment forms.

Unlike buying, there is no shelter investment requirement when you rent. In addition to saving the down payment required to buy shelter, renters also do not have the settlement costs that are involved in buying and selling a house.

Renters do not have the long-term commitment to save regularly that homeowners have taken on through long-term financing of their home purchase. However, when the monthly cost to rent is less than to own, renters also have this same opportunity to save regularly. When these savings can be invested along with the savings from initial costs of ownership, returns while renting can be attractive.

How much should you spend for shelter?

Whether you buy or rent, you must consider the proportion of your income you want to spend for shelter. Many elements enter into the decision, varying with individuals, locations, and lifestyles. There are no hard-and-fast rules.

Commonly heard rules of thumb suggest that the average family or individual should spend about one-quarter of income for shelter (sometimes stated as "one week's pay out of every month"), and that a buyer ordinarily should look for a house within a market price two and one-half times his or her annual income. In some more expensive neighborhoods where housing is in greater demand, people may be spending up to one-third of their income for shelter.

The rules cited above do not include outlays for utilities. However, when comparing home ownership costs with rental rate quotations, it is desirable to use a concept that includes these outlays. Therefore, the term "shelter" as used in this chapter has been broadened to include utilities—heat, electricity, water, and sewerage, but excluding telephone.

Information on actual shelter expenditures obtained by the Bureau of Labor Statistics in a national survey of families and individuals in 1972 and 1973 indicates that, on the average, owners and renters spent 18 percent of their annual income on shelter, including utilities. Although housing expenditures as a proportion of total income declined during the 1940's through 1960, shelter costs have been rising recently. For renters, shelter outlays, including utilities, averaged 21 percent, but their income, on average, was 40 percent less than that of homeowners.

Those who bought new homes in 1971 and 1972 spent 20 percent of their 1973 income on shelter and utilities. The reported market value of owned homes was 1.85 times annual income for both recent buyers and all home owners. Average income for these buyers was 25 percent higher than for all home owners.

Results of the survey also indicate that higher-income families spent a smaller proportion of income on shelter than families with smaller incomes. This was true for both homeowners and renters.

How do tax benefits affect shelter costs?

If you decide to buy shelter, you may benefit by being able to deduct a part of your ownership costs when filing your income-tax return. Amounts spent for interest and taxes are deductible items in federal and many state and local returns. The amount you save will depend on your income and the amount of other expenses you have to itemize. These savings tend to lower the cost of owning. Renters do not have similar tax benefits for any portion of their shelter outlays.

How do price changes affect costs of owning or renting?

Over time, costs of shelter change in response to price change. Home-purchase prices and mortgage interest rates have moved upward in recent years, as have prop-

erty taxes, property insurance rates, and prices of maintenance and repair items and services, fuel, and utilities.

The impact of higher house prices and mortgage interest rates is felt by home buyers when they seek to establish the amount of the regular payment required to buy a
house or condominium. Once the unit is purchased, however, the monthly payment typically becomes fixed and
does not vary with future changes in purchase prices or
mortgage interest rates. In this way, recent home buyers
tend to have larger monthly mortgage payments than
home owners who bought comparable shelter in earlier
years.

Amounts for other components of home ownership costs
—taxes and insurance, maintenance and repairs, and fuel
and utilities—have increased over time as a result of price
change. Owners with comparable shelter units are affected similarly by these price changes, regardless of
when they purchased their homes. All owners experience
similar percentage increases in these components of
homeowner costs due to price change, but the increase in
dollar costs is greater for owners of larger homes than for
smaller ones.

Renters also experience the effects of price change as
landlords pass on increased costs resulting from higher
taxes, insurance rates, maintenance, repair and service
costs, and fuel and utility charges. Landlords may also
periodically adjust rental rates to reflect the current market value of shelter units, even though their monthly mortgage payments remain fixed. To the extent this is so,
renter costs will increase more over a period of years than
will costs for homeowners with fixed monthly mortgage
payments.

How does the type of shelter affect the comparison?

The type of shelter you are interested in is an important
factor affecting costs and, therefore, the decision to buy or
rent. Recent trends in the shelter market have increased

the variety of shelter types available for owning or renting. As a result, the comparison of costs and returns between buying and renting can involve similar or widely divergent shelter types.

Between 1960 and 1970, many apartment units were constructed to accommodate large numbers of young people who were entering the job market for the first time, and young couples who were setting up housekeeping but lacked the resources to buy. Many of these tenants have since acquired some savings and have started families, which make them likely candidates for home ownership. But rising construction costs and higher prices for home sites have made it more costly for them to buy. During the same period the numbers of older individuals and couples whose families were grown also increased. These factors encouraged a wider variety of shelter types. Typical is the trend toward combining the features of apartment-style living with home ownership.

Ownership of condominium and cooperative apartments is growing. Many of these units are attached townhouses or in multi-unit structures (garden-style "walk-up" apartments or elevator high-rises). In the condominium form of ownership, the owner-occupier owns a single unit within a structure and shares in the ownership of the grounds and common areas. Under the cooperative ownership plan, each owner-occupant owns a prorated share of the total project. Mobile homes offer still another option of ownership to the prospective home buyer.

Questions you should ask yourself

1. Why do you want to buy a house?
   - What are the advantages for you and your family?
   - What are the disadvantages?

2. How much can you afford to pay?
   - Will you have enough regular monthly income to make your mortgage payments, and pay real-

estate taxes, insurance premiums, utilities (heat, electricity, etc.) and maintenance and repair costs?
- How much money should you have for the down payment? Will you have enough for the "closing" costs and the costs of moving in?
- Will there be enough money left over for your other needs?

3. What kind of house do you want?
   - How many rooms do you need? How big a yard? How big a kitchen? How much storage space?
   - What kind of house and neighborhood will serve all the members of your household?

4. Is now a good time to buy?
   - Are there houses for sale in your price range?
   - Can you get a mortgage?
   - Do you have a steady job? Is your family life stable?
   - Do you have a good credit history?

Why you may want to buy a house

Owning may be better than renting for:
Meeting your housing needs . . .

- You need more space now.
- You want space to grow in the future.
- Apartments may not be available in areas where you want to live.

Pride and independence . . .

- You can live the way you want.
- You don't have to depend on the landlord or deal with other tenants.
- You have a place of your own.
- You may have more privacy.

A place to settle down . . .

- You're part of your community (you pay the taxes).
- You want a place of your own to raise your family.
- You don't have to worry about moving (if you make your mortgage payments on time).

A good investment . . .

- Many homes increase in value.
- Your home is worth more and more to you as you pay off your mortgage.
- Owning a house is one way to beat inflation (house and land can increase in value faster than the cost of living).

Tax benefits for owners . . .

- Mortgage interest and real-estate taxes are deductible from your income for tax purposes so you may not have to pay so much in federal income taxes.

Good financial credit . . .

- Making your mortgage payments on time builds good credit.
- With good credit it is easier to get a loan if you need one.

BUT . . .
Owning a house can also be worse than renting because of:
The financial risks . . .

- A house can lose value (especially if not kept up) and you may not be able to get your money back when it comes time to sell.
- Neighborhood quality can decrease if other owners are not keeping up their houses or there's increasing crime, more noise and traffic, etc.
- The costs of owning may go up faster than your income.

- Family problems (health, divorce, etc.) or loss of your job may keep you from paying your mortgage on time.

The long-term commitment . . .

- Mortgage payments go on for twenty or thirty years.
- Your ownership (equity) builds slowly—most payments to the lender go toward interest during the first ten to fifteen years.
- Your money is tied up for a long time (what you put into the house cannot be spent on other things).

The difficulty of moving . . .

- When you own a home, you can't just pick up and move (houses can take time to sell).
- Your home may not suit the changing needs of your family.

The hassle of home maintenance . . .

- Keeping up a home can take a lot of time and money.
- Repairs are often expensive and difficult to foresee.
- Putting off maintenance and repairs decreases the value of your property.

Other sacrifices . . .

- Buying in the suburbs may mean a second car and higher commuting costs.

- Emergency repairs or property-tax increases may force you to postpone other plans (vacation, new car, etc.)

How much can you afford to pay?

Before you go looking for a house, it's a good idea to figure out about how much you can afford.

The price you can afford depends on:

- Your present monthly income (take-home pay). Include only the amount you can count on now and in the future.
- Your other expenses (not for housing)—food, clothing, education, installment payments, car payments, life insurance, medical bills, other taxes not deducted from your paycheck, recreation, gifts, savings, other regular expenses.
- The cash you have available (for the down payment, for the closing costs, and for moving in).

First, look at what you are now spending on rent and utilities.

- To be on the safe side, you should figure that owning a house will probably be more expensive than renting (at least during the first few years).
- How much more are you willing to spend each month to own? $25? $50? $100?

To get a better idea of what you can spend each month, add up all your regular monthly expenses (not including rent and utilities) and subtract this from your take-home pay each month (net income).

- The amount you have left is what you can reasonably budget toward owning a house.
- This figure will have to be used to pay:

  Your mortgage payments

  Your real-estate taxes

  Your heat and utilities

  Your homeowner's insurance

  Your expenses for maintenance and repairs

  Any special fees

Figuring out what you can afford

An example:

- You have $1,000 take-home pay each month.
- Your regular monthly expenses, including savings, total $700 (not including rent and utilities).
- You can budget about $300 to owning a house.

The largest part of the money you spend on your home each month will probably go for mortgage payments (that is, principal and interest payments to the lender to pay off the mortgage loan).

- This portion will differ according to your location, the kind of house you buy, and the amount of your down payment.
- As a rough guide, figure that about two-thirds of your monthly housing costs will go for mortgage payments. (The rest will go for real-estate taxes, insurance, heat and utilities, repairs, etc.)

Example continued:

- You have $300 a month for your "housing budget."
- You might spend $200 on your mortgage payments ($\frac{2}{3}$ x $300 = $200).

Figure out your total mortgage payments for the year (multiply by 12).

If you then multiply this annual-mortgage-payment figure by 10, you have a rough idea of the size of loan you might get for a house.

Example continued:

- 12 months x $200 = $2,400 mortgage payment per year.
- $2,400 x 10 = $24,000.

- This is the size of the loan you can probably afford.

What do you have in cash for the down payment?

Add this figure on to the rough loan amount and you have a "safe" estimate of the price range you can afford.

- You figure you can support a mortgage loan in the $24,000 range.
- You have $3,000 cash saved up for a down payment.
- You can safely afford to pay $27,000 for a house ($24,000 + $3,000 = $27,000).

About the down payment

A large down payment has advantages:

- The larger the down payment on the house, the less you have to borrow from a lender.
- The less you have to borrow to pay for the house, the smaller will be the monthly mortgage payments.
- The larger the down payment, the easier it is to get a mortgage loan on favorable terms.

For some people, however, a smaller down payment is better:

- You may want to keep a cash reserve for unexpected expenses and for other purchases (or investments).
- A mortgage is the least expensive kind of loan you can get. Therefore, if you have limited cash for a down payment, you should take full advantage of the mortgage loan available.

If you can't or don't want to make a large down payment, you may need to get mortgage insurance.

- If a mortgage is "insured" or "guaranteed," it means the lender is protected in case you can't pay back the loan. Therefore, the lender is willing to make a larger loan because his risk is limited.
- Mortgage insurance may be obtained from the Federal Housing Administration (FHA), from the Farmers Home Administration (FmHA), or from a private mortgage insurance company.

- If you are a veteran, you can get a mortgage guarantee from the Veterans Administration (VA). Such "GI loans" require very low down payments.
- Mortgage insurance costs about $10 to $20 per month and is paid with your regular payment to the lender.
- With mortgage insurance you may need to pay only 3 to 10 percent down on the appraised value of the house. (The lender, the FHA, or the VA will decide the appraised value.)

Other "one-time" costs of buying a home

In addition to your down payment on the house, there are two other kinds of expenses you will have. They are closing costs and move-in expenses.

Closing costs can run from 2 to 10 percent of the mortgage loan amount.

Typical closing costs include:

- Payment to the lender for processing your application, getting credit checks, appraising the house, etc.
- Payment to the lender or a lawyer for legal fees (for searching the title, recording documents, etc.)
- Prepayable expenses (for example, three months' real-estate taxes in advance, hazard insurance premiums, mortgage insurance premiums, etc.)

The lender must let you know the closing costs.

- A recent federal law known as the *Real Estate Settlement Procedures Act* (RESPA) requires most lenders to give you an estimate of the closing costs you will have to pay.
- But this estimate does not cover all the items you may have to pay at the closing (for instance, prepayable expenses). Make sure you have additional funds available.

Don't forget your move-in expenses. Be sure to have enough money for:

- Moving costs (paying a moving company, renting a van or truck, etc.).
- Utility deposits and hook-up charges (to turn on your gas or electricity, or hook up your phone).
- New furnishings or appliances you may need (for instance, curtains, refrigerator, carpets).
- Redecorating costs (paint, wallpaper, etc.).
- Other purchases (lawn equipment, tools, etc.).

Be sure to set aside some money for those "extras" you didn't count on.

What you can afford—another look

One rule of thumb that lenders and real-estate brokers often use is that the average buyer can afford to pay about two or two and one-half times his yearly take-home income for a house.

An example:

- Your annual take-home pay is $12,000.
- You can afford a house in the $24,000 to $30,000 price range (2 to 2½ x $12,000 = $24,000 to $30,000).

Be careful when you use this rule of thumb. What you can afford will depend on:

- What your other expenses are (not for housing).
- The house you're thinking of buying (a "less expensive" older home may cost you more each month than a "more expensive" newer home because of higher heating and repair expenses).
- The size of your family.
- The size of your down payment. A larger down payment means lower monthly mortgage payments.

A useful guide would be:
Use "2 times yearly income" whenever . . .

- You don't have much money for a down payment.
- You have heavy debts (e.g., car payments, college tuition, etc.).
- You plan to buy an older home that needs a lot of repairs.
- You have a large family.
- Property taxes in the neighborhood are high.
- Your income is irregular or your job picture is uncertain.
- Your job may force you to move unexpectedly.
- You have to drive a long way to get to work.

Use "2½ times yearly income" if . . .

- You plan to make a large down payment.
- You have few debts.
- You plan to buy a newer home that needs little upkeep.
- You have a small family.
- Property taxes in the neighborhood are low and will remain low.
- You are fairly sure that your income will increase in the future.
- You can do a lot of the maintenance and repairs yourself.
- You are willing to give up other things to pay for your home.

Before you look for a house, figure out what kind of house you want:

How much room do you need?

- Number of bedrooms and bathrooms
- Size of kitchen (large or small)
- Size of living room
- Other rooms you need (dining room, laundry, den, workshop, etc.)

- Amount of storage space, closets, and so forth
- Play areas for children, yard space
- Garage or parking space

Do you want to live in the city?

Possible Advantages
- Convenience?
- Lower-priced houses?
- Public transportation?

Possible Disadvantages
- Higher taxes?
- Less yard space?
- More noise or litter?

. . . or the suburbs?

- More yard space?
- Less pollution?
- Peace and quiet?

- Commute to work?
- Fewer public services?
- Higher-priced houses?

Do you want a new house?

- More efficient use of space?
- Easier to take care of?
- Less space for the money?
- Higher taxes?

. . . or an older house?

- More space for the money?
- Lower taxes?
- Harder to take care of?
- More repairs?
- More expensive to heat or cool?

Do you want a single-family house?

- More privacy?
- Less upkeep?
- No tenant headaches?
- No rental income?

. . . or one with rental units?

- Additional income; shared expenses?
- Greater responsibility and upkeep?
- Harder to find reliable tenants and deal with tenant problems?

. . . or a condominium (you own one apartment in a building complex and share the common areas with other owners)?

- Less maintenance to worry about?
- Convenience of location?
- Use of common facilities (pool, parking, etc.)?
- Better security?
- Less privacy?
- No private yard space?
- Maintenance fees?

In each case, you must decide whether the advantages outweigh the disadvantages. You (and your family) must be the judge of what is best for you.

Is now a good time to buy?

1. Do you have enough cash?
   - Money for the down payment?
   - Money for the closing costs?
   - Money for move-in costs?
   - Money for emergencies?

2. Is your job and family situation stable?
   - Steady source of income?
   - Stable family situation (health, size of family, marital situation)?

   Changes in your job or family can make it harder for you to pay for the house.

3. Is your credit good?
   - Good history of credit payments?
   - Good credit references?
   - Old debts cleared up now?

   Good credit makes it easier to get the mortgage you want.

4. Is it a buyer's or a seller's market?
   - Few buyers and lots of houses = "buyer's market" (you can bargain for a good buy).

- Lots of buyers and few houses for sale = "seller's market" (you have to compete with other buyers, may have to pay more).

5. Is financing available?
   - When lenders have money to loan, mortgage terms are more attractive.
   - "Tight money" means it is harder to get a loan (you may pay higher interest rates or a larger down payment).

6. Are there special opportunities?
   - Lots of new houses for sale?
   - Homesteading ("Handyman Specials")?
   - Homeowner subsidy programs?

Chapter 2

Finding a House

Neighborhood choice

Choosing the right neighborhood is an important part of
buying a house because . . .

1. The price you pay for a house is influenced by
   the quality of the neighborhood in which it's lo-
   cated.
   - The value of other houses in the area
   - The quality of schools and other public serv-
     ices
   - The appearance of the neighborhood (parks,
     trees, landscaping)
   - The absence of crime, vandalism, litter, noise,
     or other problems

2. The location of the house determines whether
   you will be close to the things you want or need.
   - Present or future job
   - Good schools, shopping, medical facilities
   - Convenient public transportation
   - Child-care facilities
   - Other neighborhood services

3. Your enjoyment of the house may depend on
   whether you like your neighbors and feel comfortable with them.
   - Relatives and friends in the neighborhood
   - Other children for your kids to play with

- Neighbors who share your interests
- Neighbors willing to work toward making the neighborhood better

4. The future of the neighborhood may affect the value of your house (and later your ability to sell it).
   - The value of your house will rise as the neighborhood becomes a more attractive place to live.
   - Neighborhood decline (poorly maintained homes, increasing crime, litter, vandalism, vacant houses, etc.) will lessen the value of your home.

The following list of questions will help you in choosing a neighborhood to live in:

What to consider in a neighborhood

General neighborhood quality:

- Are homes in the area well taken care of?
- Are there good public services (police, garbage collection, water, sewers, street lights, and so forth)?
- Is the neighborhood pleasant to look at?
- Is the neighborhood safe?
- Are there good schools for your children? How far away?
- Are there other aspects of the neighborhood that might bother you (factories, heavy traffic, noise, litter, smoke, and so forth)?

Convenience of the neighborhood:

- How far will you be from your present job or from places you could work?
- How far will you be from grocery shopping, stores, schools, etc.?
- Is regular public transportation available nearby?
- Are there child-care services available nearby?

- Are you near other services you might need (hospitals, doctors, etc.)?
- Are there parks or play areas nearby?

Friends, relatives, and neighbors:

- Do any of your friends or relatives live in the area now?
- Are there other children for your kids to play with?
- Will you feel comfortable with the neighbors?
- Are there active community groups that are working to improve the neighborhood?

Changes in the neighborhood (ask the people who live there now):

- Are houses and other buildings being fixed up? Or are they run down?
- Are all the houses on the block occupied or are some vacant and boarded up?
- Are longtime residents staying or are they leaving the area?
- Are major stores in the area doing well or going out of business?
- Is crime in the area getting worse or is it less of a problem now?
- Are real-estate taxes increasing? Decreasing? Will they be?
- Are home prices increasing, decreasing, or staying the same?

Looking for houses for sale

The following tips can help you find the right house:

1. Know what you are looking for.
   - Rough idea of price you can afford
   - The kind of house you want
   - General location or neighborhood
   - Things you want in a neighborhood

2. Take your time (don't be pushed into a quick decision).
   - Visit as many houses as possible to compare prices and features.
   - You will want to look at some houses two or three times.
   - Don't give in to pressure to "buy now," if you're not sure.
   - Your feelings about a house or neighborhood can change over time.
   - Think it over (but don't risk losing the house you want by waiting too long).

3. Check all important sources of information.
   - Friends and relatives
   - Real-estate brokers
   - Newspapers
   - People at work
   - Neighborhood residents
   - Supermarket bulletin boards
   - Community organizations
   - City Hall (about taxes, schools, etc.)
   - Lenders in the area (for recent sales prices, etc.)

4. Be thorough in your search.
   - Make as many visits as necessary.
   - Inspect the house during the day and at night (and when it's raining, if possible).
   - Don't rely on one source of information alone.
   - Get a professional inspection if you're not sure.
   - Don't be fooled by "cosmetics" (quick paint jobs, wallpaper, or fancy fixtures).

5. If there's something you don't know about or can't understand, make sure to ask. It's your money.

Using a real-estate broker

Real-estate brokers can help you find the right house, if you're prepared to use their services wisely.

1. Check the broker's reputation.
   - Is he or she licensed to sell real estate (ask to see the license)?
   - Is he or she a member of a reputable professional organization?

2. Visit several brokers to find out what's available in your price range.

3. Let the brokers know what you want in a house.
   - Tell them what you can afford.
   - Let them know what's important to you in a house and neighborhood.
   - Be as clear as possible to save time.

4. Get all the information.
   - Ask to see the "listing book."
   - Make copies of the information for the house you're interested in.
   - Make sure the broker tells you about all the houses in your price range.
   - Visit as many houses as necessary.

5. When visiting a house, ask questions.
   - Honest brokers will tell you about the faults of a house as well as its good points, but you'll have to ask the right questions.
   - If the broker doesn't know the answers, make sure he or she gets the information for you.
   - Don't overlook important details the broker may have forgotten to mention.
   - Check the broker's information with the owner of the house (if possible).

6. Don't be pressured into buying the first time you see a house.

- Watch out for statements like "You'd better make an offer today; another family wants this house."
- It may be true, but resist. There are other houses.
- You don't pay the broker anything for showing you houses.

7. Remember, brokers get paid a percentage of the sales price.
   - It is their job to negotiate for the highest price that you will pay and the lowest price the owner will accept.
   - The brokers work for themselves and the seller (not for you).

Dealing with discrimination while looking for a house

Discrimination takes many forms. The federal Fair Housing Law makes it illegal for anyone to discriminate because of your race, religion, sex, color, or national origin. (In many states other forms of discrimination may also be illegal.)

How discrimination may affect you:

- You may be denied a chance to look at or buy a particular house in a particular neighborhood.
- You may be "steered" by real-estate brokers into looking at houses only in certain neighborhoods.
- You may be pressured into paying more for a house than others would.
- You may become so discouraged that you decide not to buy at all.

Discrimination is sometimes hard to detect. Some of the ways it is practiced include:

- You are told the house is sold when it is not.
- You are told there are other offers, or there is no one to show you the house.

- You are asked to leave your phone number, and if the exchange is located in a minority area, no one calls you back.
- You are told the seller has decided not to sell or has raised the price.
- The broker says he or she has nothing available in your price range, and refuses to show you the listing of houses for sale.
- There is no one in the office to show you the house; you can't get an appointment; or the broker cancels an appointment.
- You are told the house isn't what you want, is too expensive, or not desirable.
- The owner is out, sick, sleeping, etc.

You should get help if you think you have been discriminated against.

What to do if you think you have been discriminated against:

1. Write down a few notes on the way you think discrimination may have been practiced:
   - The names of the real-estate agency, the seller, or other persons you think discriminated against you.
   - The date, time, and place it occurred.
   - How you think you were discriminated against.
   - The names of any witnesses who were with you when the discrimination occurred.

2. Call the people who can help. Get in touch with your local civil rights organization or the local office of the U.S. Department of Housing and Urban Development (HUD). The steps they take on your behalf usually include:
   - Taking down the facts of your case (over the phone or in person).
   - Sending out an investigator ("tester") to check whether your rights were denied in any way.

- If they agree you were discriminated against, contacting the seller, real-estate broker, or other persons involved to work out an agreement.
- If they can't work out an agreement, or if the person denies having discriminated, beginning the legal process for filing a formal complaint before the state civil rights commission or the state or federal courts.

Remember: If you think you have been discriminated against, you can and should do something about it.

Choosing the right house

Choosing the right house is important because:

1. A house is a major financial investment.
   - You may need a lot of money for the down payment, for closing costs, and for move-in expenses.
   - Much of your monthly income may have to go for your mortgage payments, and for real-estate taxes, insurance, utilities (gas, electricity, heat), and repairs.
   - If you don't choose carefully, you may lose money when it comes time to sell your house.

2. You may be living in your house a long time.
   - Make sure the rest of your family is happy with the choice.
   - Be prepared for the increasing costs of owning your home (rising taxes, higher utility bills and insurance premiums, and maintenance costs).
   - Plan for future members of your family and their changing needs.

3. You have to maintain the house.
   - What condition is the house in now?
   - If major repairs are necessary, do you have the time, money, and skills to do them yourself, or

will you have to hire someone to do them for
you?
- Over the long run is the house going to need a
lot of expensive upkeep? Will you be able to
afford it?

Keep these points in mind as you start your search for a
home.

What to look for in a house

When you visit a house for sale, you must decide if the
price is right.
Who decides a fair sales price?

- You do. You know what you want in a house and
how much you can afford.
- The seller who decides how much he will accept
for the house.
- The real-estate broker who wants the house to sell
for the highest price possible (the commission is
based on the sales price).
- Appraisers who determine the value of the property.

Remember: Sellers will almost always ask for more than
they are willing to accept. But only you can decide how
much you want to pay.
What is real value?

- Land (lot size) and landscaping
- Size of house
- Number, size of rooms/bathrooms
- Size of kitchen, amount of storage space
- Basement, attic, screened-in porches
- Quality of construction (inside/outside)
- New or upgraded electrical plumbing, heating/
cooling systems
- Energy-saving features (storm windows, insula-
tion, heat pumps)
- New roof, gutters, siding
- Convenient location, nice neighborhood

What is not real value?

- Carpeting or fancy wallpaper that may hide defects
- Owner's furnishings or appliances
- Fancy light or bathroom fixtures
- Cheap paint job, inside/outside
- Equipment you don't want or need (old washing machine, broken stove)
- Sentimental attachments of the present owner ("I've lived here all my life . . ." "I really don't want to sell the house . . ." etc.).

Real value determines the price of a house. Make sure you are paying for real value.

How to evaluate the condition of a house

When you visit a house for sale, you should inspect it carefully for . . .

- The features you want and need.
- The important faults or defects that may create problems for you now or in the future.
- How much it will cost you to own and maintain.

Remember, if you buy the house, you will have to live with your mistakes. So be careful and take your time.

The list of inspection items on the following pages will help you evaluate the condition of houses you look at.

If you are unsure about any aspect of the house, it's a good idea to get the help of a professional inspector.

- Often an inspector can point out things about the house you might not know about otherwise (like how long a roof will last, or whether you might need to replace a water heater).
- An inspector can show you structural problems or unsafe features you might overlook yourself.
- A professional inspector should also be able to evaluate the technical aspects of the house (like

whether the plumbing or electrical wiring is in good shape).
- If you are thinking of buying an older home, a professional inspection may be even more important.

The money you spend now for an inspection can save you from costly and unexpected repairs later on.

Inspecting the outside of the house

Make sure to check the following items:

1. Foundation: Check for holes, cracks, unevenness.
2. Brickwork: Look for cracks, loose or missing mortar.
3. Siding (clapboards, shingles, etc.): Look for loose or missing pieces, lifting or warping.
4. Paint: Look for peeling, chipping, blistering, etc.
5. Entrance porch: Examine steps, handrails, posts, etc., for loose or unsafe features.
6. Windows/screens: Look for cracked or broken glass, holes in screens.
7. Storm windows (northern climates): Are they complete? Are they secure and properly caulked?
8. Roof: Look for worn or bald spots; ask how old and if under warranty or not.
9. Gutters and downspouts: Check for missing sections, gaps or holes in joints. Are there signs of leaks?
10. Chimney: Look for tilting, loose or missing bricks.
11. Walls and fences: Look for holes, loose or missing sections, rotted posts.
12. Garage (if separate from house): Check doors, roof, siding, windows.
13. Driveway and sidewalks: Look for holes and cracks.

14. Grounds/landscaping: Locate property line. Are trees, shrubbery, and grass in good shape?
15. Proper drainage: Will rain (or snow) flow away from the house? Are there any problems with leaching fields or septic tanks?

When you are inside the house, check the major "systems" of the house (plumbing, electrical, etc.) and all the rooms:

1. Structure of the house: Does the house feel solid? (Jump up and down on the floors.) Check support posts and floor supports in basement; look for looseness, bending, rot, or termites.
2. Floors: Check for levelness, bowing, movement when you walk on them.
3. Stairs: Look for loose treads; loose handrails.
4. Plumbing system: Check water pipes and sewer lines for leaking or rusting; flush all toilets; turn on faucets to test the water pressure; look for clogged or sluggish drains, dripping faucets.
5. Heating system: Find out what type of heat (warm air, hot water, electrical, or steam) and what type of fuel is used. How much does it cost to heat (get last year's fuel bills)? Find out when system was last serviced.
6. Hot-water heater: Check for signs of leaking or rusting. What is the capacity or "recovery rate" (should be a minimum of thirty gallons for family of four; more for larger families)? How old is it?
7. Electrical system: Look at the "service box"— are there fuses or circuit breakers? Is it old or new? Look for exposed wires and signs of water.
8. Cooling/air conditioning: What kind of cooling is there? What is the age and condition? Is the unit under warranty? How much did it cost to use last year?
9. General layout: Are the rooms conveniently located? What are the "traffic patterns"?

10. Kitchen: What appliances are included (stove, refrigerator, dishwasher, garbage disposal)? Check for age, workability. Are there enough shelves and counter space? Are there enough electrical outlets? Are there leaks under the sink?

11. Bathrooms: Are there enough for your family? Check for cracks in tiles, signs of leaks, how long it takes to get hot water, proper ventilation (window or fan).

12. Living room/dining room: Are they large enough? Is there a fireplace? If so, does the damper work? Has the chimney been cleaned out recently?

13. Bedrooms: Are there enough for your family? Are they large enough? Does each have a window to the outside? Does each have a closet large enough for your needs?

14. Storage space: Are there enough closets in the house? Are there other rooms you can use to store things?

15. Windows: Check for broken sash cords, loose frames, locks.

16. Doors: Do they close properly? Are there good locks?

17. Walls/ceilings: Check for major cracks, loose or falling plaster, signs of leaks or stains.

18. Basement (if present): Check for signs of leaks, dampness, or flooding. Make sure there's enough lighting.

19. Attic (if accessible): Look for signs of roof leaks. Check insulation (how much? what type?). Are there signs of squirrels or other rodents?

Whenever you look at a house, don't forget to . . .

- Bring a flashlight to look into those dark corners.
- Ask if you will need a termite inspection. This may

be required by the lender, the FHA, the VA, or
your local building department.
- Ask about other inspections that may be required
  by state or local laws (in some cases sellers may
  have to pay for these). The broker or lender can tell
  you which ones are required and whether you
  should pay for them.
- Ask about warranties on any items (such as roof,
  new appliances, hot-water heater, furnace, air conditioning).
- Ask about builders' warranties on new homes
  (what is covered and for how long).
- Get a professional inspection if you have any
  doubts.

Figuring out how much the house will cost you

Once you have found a house you like, visit the house two
or three times to make sure it has everything you want
(and not too many problems). Then take the following
steps to figure out how much it will cost you to buy and
own the home.

1. Is the asking price "firm" or can you get it for
   less?
   - Never accept the asking price automatically,
     especially if the house has been for sale a long
     time.
   - If the broker doesn't give you a firm figure, start
     by taking off at least 10 percent.
   - You may be able to take off more if there are a
     lot of problems with the house.

2. Figure out your down payment.
   - With a conventional loan and no mortgage in-
     surance the down payment will be about 20 to
     25 percent of the sales price.
   - With private mortgage insurance the down pay-
     ment will be 5 to 10 percent.

- With FHA insurance the down payment may be 3 to 10 percent.
- With a VA-guaranteed loan the down payment may be less than 3 percent.

Be sure to set aside enough for closing costs (about 5 percent of the sales price) and for move-in expenses.

3. Figure out what you need for a loan (mortgage amount).
   - Subtract your down payment from the "rough" sales price.
   - What you have left is the amount you need for a loan.

4. Figure out your monthly payments to the lender.
   - These include:
     Principal and interest on the loan
     Real-estate taxes
     Mortgage insurance premium
     Homeowner's insurance—fire, theft, liability, etc.
   - For a rough estimate of principal, interest, and mortgage insurance, take 10 percent of your mortgage and divide this by 12 to get your monthly cost.
   - To be more exact, ask the broker or lender, or see the chapter on mortgages.
   - Add on your real-estate taxes (ask the broker, the seller, or the city or county assessor's department).
   - Add on homeowner's insurance (the broker or insurance company can tell you).

5. Add up the other costs: your other monthly housing costs (utilities, maintenance and repair, special fees).
   - Utilities: For an older house, get last year's figures for gas, oil, electricity, water, sewer, etc., from the seller or broker. Add 10 percent for rising costs. For a new house, ask the builder

and check with utility companies for an estimate.
- Maintenance and repairs: set aside at least 10
percent of the mortgage payment (maybe more
for older homes).
- Special fees: These may include special town
assessments, homeowner's association dues,
etc. Ask the broker, seller, or builder.

6. Add up all the monthly costs you have figured,
including your payments to the lender and your
other monthly costs.

Can you afford to pay these costs each month? Will you
have enough left over for your other expenses?

Can you afford to buy the house?

Now that you know about how much you'll be paying for
the house, and how much it will cost you each month to
own . . . How do these figures compare with your housing
budget?

- Would you be paying more than two to two and
one-half times your yearly income for the house?
- Would your monthly housing costs be more than
one-third of your monthly take-home pay?
- Your annual income (take-home pay) is $12,000; a
$27,000 house is a little more than two times your
income.
- Your monthly take-home pay is $1,000. Your
monthly housing cost ($360) is a little more than
one-third of your take-home pay.
- You may want to reduce your monthly expenses
by: getting a longer-term mortgage, making a larger
down payment, getting a lower price from the
seller, or cutting out other expenses (other than
housing).

Don't get in over your head.

- If you have a lot of extra bills (car payments, educational expenses, etc.) your housing costs should be lower.
- If you have only a few bills to pay you may be able to afford slightly higher housing costs per month.

Now that you have an idea of how much the house will cost, you are better prepared for the next step: negotiating the sales price and signing a purchase contract.

Negotiating the sales price

Once you have found a house you like (and think you can afford) you are ready to negotiate a price with the seller (or the broker).

Before you make an offer . . .

1. Know the house (and its problems).
   - Go over your housing-inspection check list.
   - You can use the "problems" of a house to bargain for a lower price.
   - Find out how much other homes on the block have sold for recently. (If yours is the most expensive, it may be harder to sell later on.)

2. Know your limits.
   - Set a definite limit for the highest price you are willing to pay.
   - Your limit should reflect what you have for a down payment and what you can spend each month for housing.

3. Know the seller's situation.
   - Is the owner eager to sell? (If so, he may accept a lower price.)
   - How long has the house been for sale? (The longer it's been for sale, the more eager the owner may be to sell.)
   - Are you competing with other buyers? (Are they "real," or is the seller/broker making them

up to get you to act in a hurry or make a higher offer?)

Making your first offer . . .

- Your first offer should be well below your limit. (If there is a broker involved, he or she should tell you if your offer is way out of line.)
- The seller should respond within a short period of time (two to three days).
- If the seller rejects your offer, he may make a "counter offer"—that is, indicate a price (less than the asking price) he would accept.
- Based on this new price range (between what you offer and what the seller will accept) refigure your housing costs. Can you still afford the house?

Making your final offer . . .

- Be sure you don't go beyond your limits. (If you do, you may run into trouble later on.)
- If the seller still refuses, be patient. He may come down in price later on, and there are other houses you will like and can afford.
- If the seller accepts your price, get it into writing as soon as possible.

Signing the purchase agreement

When you and the seller have agreed on the price, some form of *purchase agreement* will be drawn up. A purchase agreement is a legal contract in which a seller agrees to sell, and a buyer agrees to buy, a piece of property. The terms and conditions of the sale are spelled out in writing and the agreement is signed by both buyer and seller.

Purchase agreements are also called "Purchase and Sales Agreements" (P&S), "Sales Agreements," "Contracts of Purchase," "Agreements of Sale," etc., depending on the state or locality.

Before you sign an agreement to buy a house . . .

- Get the advice of a lawyer. Because a purchase agreement is a legal contract that binds you to all the terms, you should get the advice of a real-estate attorney. (He or she can also represent you at the closing.)
- Negotiate the terms, especially the sales price (also the amount of the deposit or down payment, the date of sale, what the seller has to do before you buy the house, etc.).
- Know exactly what the agreement says. Read the agreement carefully several times, and consult a real-estate lawyer or a housing counseling agency.
- Be realistic. Don't agree to terms you can't live with (such as a large down payment or buying the seller's refrigerator).
- Be thorough. Make sure everything you want is in the agreement. You may not get a chance to correct your mistakes.
- Take your time. Don't give in to pressure to sign "right now"—especially if you're not sure about the house, or the terms of the agreement.

Remember: the wording and terms of a "standard purchase agreement" can be changed as long as both you and the seller consent to the changes.

Key provisions of a purchase agreement

A purchase agreement protects you because . . .

- You know the price of the house (the seller can't change his mind).
- You know what's included in the sale (house, land, fixtures, appliances, etc.).
- You know the date of the sale ("closing") and when you can move into the house.
- You know under what conditions you can get out of the agreement and get your deposit back (for example, not getting the mortgage terms you need).

But you have to know what the agreement says. Look for these terms and conditions in your purchase agreement:

- The name(s) and address of the seller(s) (owner) and buyer (you).
- Description of the property (does it match what you think you're buying?).
- The price of the house (do you agree?).
- Amount of mortgage you need to buy the house (interest rate, number of years to repay).
- The amount of your deposit ("earnest money") and who holds it until the closing.
- The date and time of the closing (when the seller passes title to you and you become the owner).
- Where the closing will take place.
- Provision to extend the closing date (if you or the seller can't meet the terms of the agreement).
- Provision for disposition of deposit if something goes wrong.
- Amount of the broker's fee (if any). (Seller has to pay this.)
- Adjustments to be made at the closing (for example, taxes already paid by the seller, fuel adjustments, "points" paid by seller or buyer).
- Details of what is included in the sale (carpets, appliances, curtains, light fixtures, etc.).
- Special conditions of the sale (for example, seller will repair broken windows, pay for a termite inspection and treatment, etc.).
- Inspections you can make before closing (and, if reports aren't favorable, will allow you to cancel the agreement).
- Property easements. (The seller must tell you if anyone else has the right to use your land.)

Remember: Don't sign a purchase agreement until you and the seller agree on all the terms.

Making a deposit on the house

When you sign the purchase agreement, you will probably have to make an *earnest money* deposit on the house.

What is earnest money for? Earnest money is a cash deposit given to the broker (or the seller's lawyer) that binds you and the seller to the terms of the purchase agreement. The deposit you make when you sign the purchase agreement will be applied to your down payment on the house when you become the owner at the closing. An example:

- You have agreed to pay $27,000 for the house.
- You pay $500 now as earnest money to "bind" the purchase agreement.
- You expect to make a $1,400 down payment on the house.
- At the closing you must pay the difference between your deposit and the down payment ($1,400 less $500 deposit = $900).

How much should the deposit be?

- As little as possible. Hold on to as much of your down payment as possible until the sale is completed. (Deposits can be hard to get back if something goes wrong.)
- The broker or the seller will usually tell you what he feels is a reasonable amount.
- Deposits can be as little as $100 or as much as the full down payment.
- If your deposit is less than the down payment, you must pay the difference at the closing.

Who should hold the deposit?

- The broker, the seller's lawyer, or a "third party" who will be responsible for the money until the sale is completed.
- The seller should not hold the deposit.

Can the deposit be returned to you if something goes wrong?

- Yes, if the seller does not live up to the terms of the agreement, or if you cannot get the financing you need, or if the inspections uncover major defects. (You and your lawyer should be sure this is spelled out in the purchase agreement.)
- But if you back out of the sale for reasons not provided for in the agreement, then the seller may be allowed to keep your deposit.

Remember: Never make a deposit without a written agreement that spells out the terms of the sale. Never sign a purchase agreement without consulting a real-estate lawyer.

Signing other agreements

A purchase agreement is the basic contract that binds you and the seller to the terms of the sale. However, there are other written agreements you may run into.

1. Offer to purchase (binder).
   - This is often a first step before signing a purchase agreement.
   - You make a formal, written offer to buy the house at a given price (and you sign and date the offer).
   - You make a small earnest-money deposit to show the seller you are serious about the deal.
   - If the seller accepts the offer, he also signs it and agrees to the sale. However, the offer is valid only if you and the seller sign a purchase agreement within a certain number of days.
   - The advantage of the offer to you is that the price of the house is fixed and you can negotiate the other terms of the sale in the purchase agreement. (Also, you need less money for the deposit.)

  - The disadvantage is that it is another step that takes time.

2. Option to buy.
  - An option to buy gives you an exclusive right to buy a piece of property for a certain price within a certain time period (for example, six months).
  - You pay the owner of the property a small percentage of the sales price (3 to 10 percent) for the right to buy the property.
  - If you buy the property within the time allowed, the price you paid for the option is subtracted from the down payment.
  - If you don't buy the property within the time allowed, you lose your option to buy (and the money you paid for it.).

3. Right of first refusal.
  - If the owner is not sure he wants to sell, he may give you a *right of first refusal*.
  - This means that if he does decide to sell and gets a serious offer from someone else, you have the right to buy the property at that same price.

4. Personal-property agreements.
  - It's often better for you to write up a separate agreement about any of the seller's personal property you want to buy (such as a washing machine, air conditioner, furniture, etc.), rather than include them in the purchase agreement.
  - You don't want to lose the house because of a disagreement or misunderstanding about furniture!

Chapter 3

Closing and Settlement

Before you go to the closing, ask yourself:

- Are all necessary inspections done?
- Are all required repairs completed?
- Is your lawyer satisfied that title to the property is clear?
- Have you an insurance policy or binder on the home? Will it be in effect on the day you close?
- Do you know how much the closing costs will be?
- Do you have a certified check to pay for the closing costs?
- Do you have the right time, date, place of the closing?

The closing process

What to do before the closing:

- Inspect the house one more time to make sure everything is the way you expect it to be. If there has been any damage to the property the seller must fix it before the closing. (Your purchase agreement should clearly state this.)
- Make sure the seller (and all his furnishings and trash) will be out of the house before your closing date. But remember, it's better not to let a house remain empty for too long.
- Call your mover to confirm the moving date. Find out if he needs a deposit, and make sure you will have enough money to pay him.

- Give your present landlord plenty of notice (at least thirty days). Check your lease.
- Notify the gas, electric, phone, and fuel companies of your move so they can shut off service in your present home and turn it on in your new one.
- Check with the lender (or closing agent) to find out how much money you will need for "closing needs." Federal law entitles you to know at least twenty-four hours before the closing what charges you will have to pay, including those that were not disclosed on your RESPA statement from the lender.
- Check with your lawyer to make sure he or she can go along with you to the closing (unless you are represented by a title insurance company).

Be sure you have . . .

- The right time, date, and place of the closing.
- A paid insurance policy (or binder) for the house.
- Any receipts for other items you may already have paid for, such as your deposit on the house, mortgage application fees, or inspection fees.
- Enough money for all the closing costs (it's wise to bring more than the lender says) in a certified check.

What is a closing?

A typical closing is a meeting between the buyer(s), seller(s), representatives or agents for the lender (and title insurance company in some cases), and the real-estate broker. The purpose of the meeting is to transfer title (ownership) of the property from the seller to you, the buyer.

In some states the broker may represent both you and the seller, or the closing process may be handled by an *escrow agent.*

What happens at the closing?

- The lender's agent will ask for your paid insurance policy (or binder) on the house.
- The agent will list the adjustments (what you owe the seller: remainder of the down payment, pre-paid taxes, etc.; and what the seller owes you: unpaid taxes, prepaid rents, etc.).
- You will sign the mortgage or *deed of trust* (the legal document giving the lender the right to take back your property if you fail to make your mortgage payments).
- You will also sign the *mortgage note* (the promise to repay the loan in regular monthly payments of a certain amount).
- You will then be "loaned" the money to pay the seller for the house.
- The *title* (proof of ownership of the property) passes from the seller to you, usually in the form of a deed (the document that transfers the title) signed by the seller.
- The lender's agent will collect the closing costs from you, and give you a *loan disclosure statement* (a list of all the items you have paid for). Be sure to keep this.
- The deed and mortgage will then be recorded (put on file) in the town or county Registry of Deeds.

Now that you know what happens at a closing, you'll want to know what it costs.

Closing costs can be expensive

The amount of closing costs differs from place to place.

- Closing costs can add as much as 2 to 10 percent to the cost of buying your home. Example:
  A $30,000 house may have closing costs ranging from $600 to $3,000.
- Federal law requires your lender to provide you with a *good faith estimate* of your closing costs.

Normally, you will receive this soon after your loan application has been submitted to the lender (RESPA).

Closing costs include lawyer's fees, title insurance, mortgage application fees, appraisal fees, real-estate taxes, and other costs over the purchase price of the property. Some typical items are:

- Legal fees — what the lender charges for preparing and recording legal documents, searching the title, and other services performed to protect the lender's interests.
- Origination fee — lender's charge to make the loan (usually 1 percent of the mortgage).
- Appraisal fees — charge by the lender for an inspection of the property to determine its value. (FHA and VA appraisal fees are fixed by law.)
- Inspection fees — cost of any other inspections required by local housing codes, government agencies, or individual lenders, such as termite or lead-paint inspections (if you haven't already paid for them yourself).
- Mortgage insurance — fee to the company or government agency that insures the loan in case you fail to make your payments.
- Credit report — all lenders require a credit history of the buyer; this may be included in the application fee.
- Application fee — the charge by the lender for processing your loan application.
- Survey fees — the lender may require a registered survey or a map showing the location of the house and the boundaries of the property.

There may also be . . .

- Real-estate taxes or town service charges (which might include a special assessment for new sidewalks or sewer improvements, for example). These are paid in advance and held in a special impound or escrow account by the lender.
- Home insurance and mortgage insurance premiums paid several months in advance and also held by the lender.
- Interest charges from the date of the closing to the date of your first mortgage payment.

These advance payments are called prepayable items and will also appear on your loan disclosure statement.

When you have paid all the closing costs, and when the deed and mortgage are recorded, get the keys from the seller—you now own the home.

Check Appendix A for the following definitions:

- assessment
- escrow
- impound
- prepayables, points, etc.

Settlement costs

For many people, buying a home is the single most significant financial step of a lifetime. The Real Estate Settlement Procedures Act (RESPA), a federal statute, helps to protect you at this step.

Settlement is the formal process by which ownership of real property passes from seller to buyer. It is the end of the home-buying process, the time when title to the property is transferred from the seller to the buyer.

RESPA covers most residential mortgage loans used to finance the purchase of one to four family properties, such as a house, a condominium or cooperative apartment unit, a lot with a mobile home, or a lot on which you will build a house or place a mobile home using the proceeds of the loan.

RESPA was not designed to set the prices of settlement services. Instead, it provides you with information to take the mystery out of the settlement process, so that you can shop for settlement services and make informed decisions.

Suppose you have just found a home you would like to buy. In a typical situation, when you reach an agreement with the seller on the price, you then sign a sales contract. The terms of the sales contract can be negotiated to your benefit, as this section explains.

Next you will probably seek a mortgage to finance the purchase. This section suggests important questions you should raise as you shop for a lender.

When you file your application for a loan, the lender is required by RESPA to provide a good-faith estimate of the cost of settlement services and a copy of the Housing and Urban Development's guide to settlement costs. The lender has three business days, after written loan application, to mail these materials to you.

Between loan application time and settlement, you usually have a chance to shop for settlement services to ensure that you will obtain good value for your money.

Finally, one business day before settlement, if you so request, the person conducting the settlement must allow you an opportunity to see a Uniform Settlement Statement that shows whatever figures are available at that time for settlement charges you will be required to pay. At settlement, the completed Uniform Settlement Statement will be given to you.

Note: In some parts of the country where there is no actual settlement meeting, or in cases where neither you nor your authorized agent attends the closing meeting, the person conducting settlement has the obligation to deliver the Uniform Settlement Statement to you by mail.

There is no standard settlement process followed in all localities; therefore, what you experience, involving many of the same services, will probably vary from the description in this section.

Shopping for services

When settlement arrives, you are committed to the purchase of the property and may have made a partial payment, sometimes called earnest money, to the seller or his agent. Services may have been performed for which you are obligated to pay. Unless a seller fails to fulfill a legally binding promise or has acted in a fraudulent fashion, you are normally obligated to complete your part of the contract and pay settlement costs. Thus the time to decide the terms of sale, raise questions, and establish fair fees is not at time of settlement services. By the time of settlement, any changes in settlement costs and purchase terms may be difficult to negotiate.

You can also negotiate with the seller of the house about who pays various settlement fees and other charges. There are generally no fixed rules about which party pays which fees, although in many cases this is largely controlled by local custom.

Among the many factors that determine the amount you will pay for settlement costs are the location of your new home, the type of sales contract you negotiate, the arrangements made with the real-estate broker, the lender you select, and your decisions in selecting the various firms that provide required settlement services. If the chosen house is located in a "special flood hazard area," identified as such on a flood insurance map, the lender may require you to purchase flood insurance pursuant to federal law.

Role of the broker

Although real-estate brokers provide helpful advice on many aspects of home buying, and may in some areas supervise the settlement, they normally serve the interests of the seller, not the buyer. The broker's basic objective is to obtain a signed contract of sale which properly expresses the agreement of the parties, and to complete the sale. However, as state licensing laws require that the broker be fair in his dealings with all parties to the t͏ransaction, you should feel free to point this out to the broker if you feel you are being treated unfairly.

A broker may recommend that you deal with a particular lender, title company, attorney, or other provider of settlement services. Ask brokers why they recommend a particular company or firm in preference to others. Advise them that while you welcome their suggestions (and, indeed, they probably have good contacts), you reserve the right to pick your own providers of services.

Negotiating a sales contract

The sales agreement you and the seller sign can expressly state which settlement costs you will pay and which will be paid by the seller, although some may be negotiable up to the time of settlement. Buyers can and do negotiate with sellers as to which party is to pay for specific settlement costs. The success of such negotiations depends upon factors such as how eager the seller is to sell and you are to buy, the quality of the house itself, how long the house has been on the market, whether other potential buyers are interested, and how willing you are to negotiate for lower costs. If the contract is silent on these costs, they are still open to negotiation.

There is no standard sales contract that you are required to sign. You are entitled to make any modification or additions in any standard form contract to which the seller will agree. You should consider including the following clauses:

- The seller provides title, free and clear of all liens and encumbrances except those which you specifically agree to in the contract or approve when the results of the title search are reported to you. You may negotiate as to who will pay for the title search service to determine whether the title is "clear."
- A refund of your deposit (earnest money) will be made by the seller or escrow agent, and cancella-

tion of the sale will occur if you are unable to secure from a lending institution a first mortgage or
deed-of-trust loan with an amount, interest rate,
and length of term, as set forth in the contract,
within a stated time period.
- A certificate will be provided at the time of settlement, stating that the house is free from termites or
termite damage.
- A certificate will be provided that the plumbing,
heating, electrical systems, and appliances are in
working order, and that the house is structurally
sound. Negotiate who pays for any necessary inspections. There is no uniform custom in most
areas. Many buyers prefer to pay for these inspections because they want to know that the inspector
is conducting the service for them, not the seller.
(You can also purchase a warranty to back up the
inspection, if you wish.)
- An agreement will be reached on how taxes, water
and sewer charges, premiums on existing transfer-
able insurance policies, utility bills, interest on
mortgages, and rent (if there are tenants) are to be
divided between buyer and seller as of the date of
the settlement.

Before you sign the sales contract, make sure that it
correctly expresses your agreement with the seller on
such important details as the sales price of the home;
method of payment; the time set for your taking possession; what fixtures, appliances, and personal property are
to be sold with the home; and the other items described
above.

The above list is not complete, but it does illustrate the
importance of the sales agreement and its terms. Before
you sign a sales contract you may want to ask an attorney
to review the proposed agreement and determine if it protects your interests, for once signed, the contract is binding on you and the seller. If you do not know an attorney,

you may wish to consult the local bar association referral service or neighborhood legal service office.

Selecting an attorney

If you seek the aid of an attorney, first ask what services will be performed for what fee. If the fee seems too high, shop for another lawyer. Does the attorney have substantial experience in real estate? The U.S. Supreme Court has said that it is illegal for bar associations to fix minimum fee schedules for attorneys, so do not be bashful about discussing and shopping for legal fees you can afford. Your attorney will understand.

Questions you may wish to ask the attorney include: What is the charge for reading documents and giving advice concerning them? For being present at settlement? Will the attorney represent any other party in the transaction in addition to you? In some areas attorneys act as closing agents handling the mechanical aspects of the settlement. A lawyer who does this may not fully represent your interests since, as closing agent, he would be representing the seller and other interests as well.

Selecting a lender

Your choice of lender will influence not only your settlement costs, but also the monthly cost of your mortgage loan.

Lending institutions require certain settlement services, such as a new survey or title insurance, or they may charge you for other settlement-related services, such as the appraisal or credit report. You may find, in shopping for a lender, that other institutions may not have such requirements.

Many lending institutions deal regularly with certain title companies, attorneys, appraisers, surveyors, and others in whom they have confidence. They may want to arrange for settlement services to be provided through these parties.

If you choose a lending institution which allows you a choice of settlement service providers, you should shop and compare among the providers in your area, to find the best service for the best price. Where the lender designates the use of particular firms, check with other firms to see if the lender's stated charges are competitive.

Questions you may want to ask the lender should include these:

- Are you required to carry life or disability insurance? Must you obtain it from a particular company? (You may prefer no insurance or may wish to obtain it at a better premium rate elsewhere.)
- Is there a late-payment charge? How much? How late may your payment be before the charge is imposed? You should be aware that late payments may harm your credit rating.
- Will the lender release you from personal liability if your loan is assumed by someone else when you sell your house?
- If you sell the house and the buyer assumes your loan, will the lender have the right to charge an assumption fee, raise the rate of interest, or require payment in full of the mortgage?
- Will you be required to pay monies into a special reserve (escrow or impound) account to cover taxes or insurance? If so, how large a deposit will be required at the closing of the sale? The amount of reserve deposits required is limited under RESPA. Some recent state laws have required that these accounts bear interest for the benefit of the borrower (buyer). If reserve requirements can be waived, you will be responsible for paying the particular charges for taxes or insurance directly to the tax collector or insurance company.

In looking for the best mortgage to fit your particular financial needs, you may wish to check the terms and requirements of a private conventional loan versus a loan insured through the Federal Housing Administration or Farmers Home Administration or guaranteed by the Veterans Administration. The FHA, VA, and Farmers Home Administration loans involve federal ceilings on permissible charges for some settlement services, which may be of interest to you. Ask lenders about these programs. Another source of information about the federally insured or guaranteed programs is from public documents.

If you are dealing with the lender who holds the existing mortgage, you might be able to take over the prior loan in a transaction called *assumption*. Assumption usually saves money in settlement costs if the interest rate on the prior loan is lower than that being asked in the market. In times of inflation in the housing market, a higher down payment might be required than if you had obtained a new loan. You may want to ask the seller whether he would be willing to "take back" a second mortgage to finance part of the difference between the assumed loan and the sales price.

Selecting a settlement agent

Settlement practices vary from locality to locality, and even within the same county or city. In various areas settlements are conducted by lending institutions, title-insurance companies, escrow companies, real-estate brokers, and attorneys for the buyer or seller. By investigating and comparing practices and rates, you may find that the first suggested settlement agent may not be the least expensive. You might save money by taking the initiative in arranging for settlement and selecting the firm and location that meet your needs.

Securing title services

A title search may take the form of an abstract, a compilation of pertinent legal documents that provides a condensed history of the property ownership and related matters. In many areas title searches are performed by extracting information from the public record without assembling abstracts. In either situation, an expert examination is necessary to determine the status of title, and this is normally made by attorneys or title-company employees. In areas where both title-insurance companies and attorneys perform these and other settlement services, compare fees for services (such as title certification, document preparation, notary fee, closing fee, etc.), provided by each to determine the better source for these services.

In many jurisdictions a few days or weeks prior to settlement the title-insurance company will issue a binder (sometimes called a *commitment to insure*) or preliminary report, a summary of findings based on the search or abstract. It is usually sent to the lender for use until the title-insurance policy is issued after the settlement. The binder lists all the defects in and liens against the title identified by the search. You should arrange to have a copy sent to you (or to an attorney who represents you) so that you can raise an objection if there are matters affecting the title that you did not agree to accept when you signed the contract of sale.

Title insurance is often required to protect the lender against loss if a flaw in title is not found by the title search made when the house is purchased. You may also get an owner's title policy to protect yourself. In some states, attorneys provide bar-related title insurance as part of their services in examining title and providing a title opinion. In these states the attorney's fee may include the title-insurance premium, although the total title-related charges in the transaction should be taken into account in determining whether you will realize any savings.

Bear in mind that a title-insurance policy issued only to the lender does not protect you. Similarly, the policy issued to a prior owner, such as the person from whom you are buying the house, does not protect you. To protect yourself from loss because of a mistake made by the title searcher, or because of a legal defect of a type that does

not appear on the public records, you will need an owner's policy. Such a mistake rarely occurs, but, when it does, it can be financially devastating to the uninsured. If you buy an owner's policy it is usually much less expensive if purchased simultaneously with a lender's policy.

To reduce title-insurance costs, be sure to compare rates among various title-insurance companies, and ask what services and limitations in coverage are provided by each policy so that you can decide whether a higher rate is consistent with your needs.

Depending upon practice in your jurisdiction, there may be no need for a full historical title search each time title to a home is transferred. If you are buying a home that has changed hands within the last several years, inquire at the title company that issued the previous title-insurance policy about a "reissue rate," which would be a lower charge than for a new policy. If the title-insurance policy of the previous owner is available, take it to the title-insurance company or lawyer whom you have selected to do your search.

To mark the boundaries of the property as set out in the title, lenders may require a survey. A home buyer may be able to avoid the cost of a repetitive complete survey of the property if he can locate the surveyor who previously surveyed the project. He can update the existing survey. However, the requirements of investors who buy loans originated by your lender may limit the lender's discretion to negotiate this point. Check with the lender or title company on this.

Good-faith estimates

When you file your application for a loan, the lender must also, under the terms of RESPA, provide you with good-faith estimates of settlement services charges you will likely incur. If he does not give them to you, he has three business days in which to put them in the mail.

The lender is required to give you his good-faith estimate, based upon his experience in the locality in which the property is located, for each settlement charge that he anticipates you will pay, except for paid-in-advance hazard insurance premium and reserves deposited with the lender. The estimate may be stated as either a dollar amount or a range for each charge. Where the lender designates the use of a particular firm, the lender must make its good-faith estimate based upon the lender's knowledge of the amounts charged by the firm. The form used for this good-faith estimate must be concise and clear, and the estimates must bear a reasonable relationship to the costs you will likely incur. If the lender provides you good-faith estimates in the form of ranges, ask the lender what the total settlement costs will most likely be. While the lender is not obligated to provide this information under RESPA, it is important information for you to know as you evaluate the different mortgage packages being offered you.

Lenders are not required to give good-faith estimates for reserves deposited with them or for the prepaid hazard insurance premium because these charges require information not normally known to the lender at time of loan application. It is important for you to make these calculations because they can represent a sizable cash payment you may have to make at settlement. Ask what the lender's policies are in terms of reserve accounts, for what items the lender requires reserves, and for what period of time. You may want to ask the lender to run through a hypothetical calculation for you based upon the date you will most likely close on the house. Other assumptions may be necessary, such as the assessed value of the property for determining property taxes. The lender can probably be more specific on hazard insurance premiums, particularly for those coverages that a lender requires.

Once you have obtained these estimates from the lender, be aware that they are only estimates. The final costs may not be the same. Estimates are subject to changing market conditions, and fees may change. Changes in the date of settlement may result in changes in escrow and proration requirements. In certain cases, it may not be possible for the lender to anticipate exactly the pricing policies of settlement firms. Moreover, your own careful choice of settlement firms might result in lower costs, just as hasty decisions might result in higher costs. Remember that the lender's estimate is not a guarantee.

Lender designation of settlement-service providers

Some lending institutions follow the practice of designating specific settlement-service providers to be used for legal services, title examination services, title insurance, or the conduct of settlement.

Where this occurs, the lender, under RESPA, is required to provide you, as part of the good-faith estimates, with a statement in which the lender sets forth:

1. The name, address, and telephone number of each provider he has designated. This must include a statement of the specific services each designated firm is to provide for you, as well as an estimate of the amount the lender anticipates you will have to pay for the service, based on the lender's experience as to what the designated provider usually charges. If the services or charges are not clear to you, ask further questions.

2. Whether each designated firm has a business relationship with the lender.

While designated firms often provide the services needed, a conflict of interest may exist. Take, for example, the situation where the provider must choose between your interests and those of the lender. Where legal services are involved, it is wise to employ your own attorney to ensure that your interests are properly protected. It is wise for you to contact other firms to determine whether their costs are competitive and their services are comparable.

Disclosure of settlement costs one day before closing and delivery

One business day before settlement, you have the right to inspect the form, called the Uniform Settlement Statement, on which the services provided to you and fees charged to you are itemized. This form (developed by the U.S. Department of Housing and Urban Development) is filled out by the person who will conduct the settlement meeting. Be sure you have the name, address, and telephone number of the settlement agent if you wish to inspect this form or if you have any questions.

The settlement agent may not have all costs available the day before closing, but is obligated to show you, upon request, what is available.

The Uniform Settlement Statement must be delivered or mailed to you (while another statement goes to the seller) at or before settlement. If, however, you waive your right to delivery of the completed statement at settlement, it will then be mailed at the earliest practicable date.

In parts of the country where the settlement agent does not require a meeting, or in cases where you or your agent does not attend the settlement, the statement will be mailed as soon as possible after settlement, and no advance inspection is required.

The Uniform Settlement Statement is not used in situations where:

1. there are no settlement fees charged to the buyer (because the seller has assumed all settlement-related expenses), or,

2. the total amount the borrower is required to pay for all charges imposed at settlement is determined by a fixed amount and the borrower is informed of this fixed amount at the time of loan application. In the latter case, the lender is required to provide the borrower, within three business days of application, an itemized list of services rendered.

Escrow closing

Settlement practices differ from state to state. In some parts of the country, settlement may be conducted by an escrow agent, which may be a lender, a real-estate agent, a title-company representative, an attorney, or an escrow company. After entering into a contract of sale, the parties sign an escrow agreement, which requires them to deposit specified documents and funds with the agent. Unlike other types of closing, the parties do not meet around a table to sign and exchange documents. The agent may request a title report and policy; draft a deed or other documents; obtain rent statements; pay off existing loans; adjust taxes, rents, and insurance between the buyer and seller; compute interest on loans; and acquire hazard insurance. All this may be authorized in the escrow agreement. If all the papers and monies are deposited with the agents within the agreed time, the escrow is "closed."

The escrow agent then records the appropriate documents and gives each party the documents and money each is entitled to receive, including the completed Uniform Settlement Statement. If one party has failed to fulfill his agreement, the escrow is not closed and legal complications may follow.

Truth-in-lending

The lender is required to provide you a Truth-in-Lending statement by the time of loan consummation, which discloses the annual percentage rate or effective interest rate that you will pay on your mortgage loan. This rate may be higher than the contract interest rate because the latter includes only interest, while the annual percentage rate includes discount points, fees, and financing charges and certain other charges besides, on the loan. The Truth-in-Lending statement will also disclose any additional charges for prepayment should you pay off the remaining balance of the mortgage before it is due.

Lenders are not required to provide you a Truth-in-Lending disclosure at the time of loan application, when the good-faith estimate of settlement costs and an informational booklet are given to you. However, since the annual percentage rate the lender will be charging you is an important item of information that you can use as you

shop for services, you may want to request its disclosure
at the time of loan application.

Protection against unfair practices

A principal finding of Congress in the Real Estate Settlement Procedures Act of 1974 is that consumers need protection from ". . . unnecessarily high settlement charges
caused by certain abusive practices that have developed
in some areas of the country." The potential problems
discussed below may not be applicable to most loan settlements, and the professionals in the settlement business
will give you good service. Nevertheless, you may save
yourself money and worry by keeping the following considerations in mind.

Kickbacks. Kickbacks and referrals of business for gain are
often tied together. The law prohibits anyone from giving
or taking a fee, kickback, or anything of value under an
agreement that business will be referred to a specific person or organization. It is also illegal to charge or accept a
fee or part of a fee where no service has actually been
performed. This requirement does not prevent agents for
lenders and title companies, attorneys, or others actually
performing a service in connection with the mortgage loan
or settlement transaction from receiving compensation for
their work. It also does not prohibit payments pursuant to
cooperative brokerage, such as a multiple-listing service,
and referral arrangements between real-estate agents and
brokers.
    The prohibition is aimed primarily at estimating the
kind of arrangement in which one party agrees to return
part of his fee in order to obtain business from the refer-
ring party. The danger is that some settlement fees can be
inflated to cover payments to this additional party, resulting in a higher total cost to you. There are criminal pen-
alties of both fine and imprisonment for any violation of
these provisions of law. There are also provisons for you
to recover three times the amount of the kickback, rebate,

or referral fee involved, through a private lawsuit. In any successful action to enforce your right, the court may award you court costs together with a fee for your attorney.

Title companies. Under the law, the seller may not require, as a condition of sale, that title insurance be purchased by the buyer from any particular title company. A violation of this will make the seller liable to you in an amount equal to three times all charges made for the title insurance.

Fair credit-reporting. There are credit-reporting agencies around the nation that are in the business of compiling credit reports on citizens, covering data such as how you pay your bills, if you have been sued or arrested, if you filed for bankruptcy, etc. In addition, this file may include your neighbors' and friends' views of your character, general reputation, or manner of living. This latter information is referred to as an "investigative consumer report."

If the terms of your financing have been adversely affected by a credit report, you have the right to inspect the summary of that report free of charge (there may otherwise be a small fee). The accuracy of the report can also be challenged, and corrections required to be made. For more detailed information on your credit report rights, contact the Federal Trade Commission (FTC) in Washington, D.C., or the nearest FTC regional office.

The right to file complaints

As with any consumer problems, the place to start if you have a complaint is back at the source of the problem (the lender, settlement agent, broker, etc.). If that initial effort brings no satisfaction and you think you have suffered damages through violations of the Real Estate Settlement Procedures Act of 1974, as amended, you may be entitled to bring a civil action in the U.S. District Court for the district in which the property involved is located, or in any other court of competent jurisdiction. This is a matter best determined by your lawyer. Any suit you file under

RESPA must be brought within one year from the date of the occurrence of the alleged violation. You may have legal remedies under other state or federal laws in addition to RESPA.

You should note that RESPA provides for specific legal sanctions only under the provisions that prohibit kickbacks and unearned fees, and that prohibit the seller from requiring the buyer to use a particular title insurer. If you feel you should recover damages for violations of any provision of RESPA, you should consult your lawyer.

Most settlement-service providers, particularly lenders, are supervised by some governmental agency at the local, state, and/or federal level. Others are subject to the control of self-policing associations. If you feel a provider of settlement services has violated RESPA, you can address your complaint to the agency or association that has supervisory responsibility over the provider.

The home buyer's obligations (repayment of loan and maintenance of home)

At settlement you will sign papers legally obligating you to pay the mortgage loan financing the purchase of your home. You must pay according to the terms of the loan— interest rate, amount and due date of each monthly payment, repayment period—specified in the documents signed by you. You will probably sign at settlement a note or bond that is your promise to repay the loan for the unpaid balance of the purchase price. You will also sign a mortgage or deed of trust, which pledges your home as security for repayment of the loan.

Failure to make monthly mortgage payments on time may lead to a late-payment charge, if provided for in the documents. If you default on the loan by missing payments altogether and do not make them up within a period of time usually set by state law, the documents also specify certain actions that the lender may take to recover the amount owed. Ultimately, after required notice to you, a default could lead to foreclosure and sale of the home that secures your loan.

You should also be careful to maintain your home in a proper state of repair, both for your own satisfaction and comfort as the occupant and because the home is security for your loan. The mortgage or deed of trust may in fact specifically obligate you to keep the property in good repair and not allow deterioration.

Read the documents carefully at or before settlement, and be aware of your obligations as a homeowner.

Chapter 4

Mortgages

Getting started

If you've been thinking about buying a home, you may wonder if it's still possible. Interest rates and purchase prices have become unpredictable. Traditional mortgages with fixed interest rates and long terms are more difficult to find.

As a result, new mortgage plans called "creative financing" are emerging. These plans represent a departure from traditional mortgages: they can involve more risk for the buyer and are frequently tied to changes in the market. But they also can make home buying possible and may offer lower interest rates.

So if you want to purchase a home, it may not be too late. But to get a mortgage that meets your needs, you should educate yourself first.

This chapter will introduce you to the new plans. Other sources of information include your state, county, or city consumer affairs office; local realtors, home builders, and lenders; bookstores; and the real-estate section of your newspaper. You may also want to consult the payment tables in Appendix B to help you calculate whether you can afford a specific loan.

Above all, shop carefully. And, as you read through this chapter, keep in mind the following:

- Don't use yesterday's assumptions about today's real-estate market.

- The key is affordability. Consider your total housing costs—including loan payments (now and in the future), maintenance, property taxes, and your anticipated income changes.
- Look into several sources of financing. You may be able to combine two or more mortgages.
- Ask questions. For example, an enthusiastic seller may not be familiar with the fine points of the financing arrangement.
- Negotiate with the seller or lender. Better terms may be available than those initially offered.
- Consider getting an attorney or a real-estate broker to represent you. This could be the largest investment of your life.
- Study all available materials about your mortgage costs. With loans from institutional lenders, the creditor is required to give you a statement of your loan costs and terms before you sign the agreement. This information will include the "annual percentage rate" (APR), which measures your total credit costs, including interest, points, and mortgage insurance.

Defining your terms

To buy or sell a home today, it's important to know the new vocabulary. Don't let terms like "amortization" or "appreciation" scare you. Understanding the new concepts can save you time and money; it can also prevent you from obtaining a mortgage ill-suited to your needs.

Three important words are *interest, principal,* and *equity.* When you first buy a home you're likely to make a down payment on the property. But, because you financed the purchase, you are now in debt and the lender "owns" most of the property's value. In traditional mortgages, the monthly payments on the loan are weighted. During the first years, they are largely interest; in time, more of each payment is credited to the loan itself, or the principal. Gradually, as you pay off principal, you build up equity, or ownership. Your equity also increases if the value of the home increases. This process of gradually obtaining equity and reducing debt through payments of principal and interest is called *amortization*.

Until recently most mortgages had fixed monthly payments, a fixed interest rate, and full amortization (or transfer of equity) over a period of twenty to thirty years. These features worked in the buyer's favor. Inflation made your payments seem less and your property worth more. So, although the payments seemed hard to meet at first, over time, it became easier.

Creative financing plans are different from traditional mortgages. They may help you buy a home you otherwise couldn't, but they also may involve greater risks for buyers. For example, the interest rate and monthly payments may change during the loan to reflect what the market will bear. Or the interest rate may fluctuate while the payments stay the same, and the amount of principal paid off may vary. The latter approach allows the lender to credit a greater portion of the payment to interest when rates are high. Some plans also offer below-market interest rates, but they may not help you build up equity.

In shopping for financing sources today, keep in mind the terms that are keys to the affordability of the home:

- the sales price minus your down payment, or amount you finance
- the length, or maturity, of the loan
- the size of the monthly payments
- the interest rate or rates
- whether the payments or rates may change
- how often and how much the payments or rates may change
- whether there is an opportunity for refinancing the loan when it matures, if necessary

These concepts will be discussed in greater detail as specific types of financing are described.

Fixed-rate mortgage

Fixed-rate mortgages have an interest rate and monthly payments that remain constant over the life of the loan. This sets a maximum on the total amount of principal and interest you pay during the loan. Traditionally, these mortgages have been long-term. As the loan is repaid, ownership shifts gradually from lender to buyer.

For example, suppose you borrow $50,000 at 15 percent for thirty years. Your monthly payments on this loan would be $632.22. Over thirty years, your total obligation for principal and interest would never exceed a fixed, pre-determined amount.

Fixed-rate mortgages are not as readily available as in the past. Because the market is highly changeable, many lenders are reluctant to lock themselves into rates that cannot adapt to new conditions.

Some lenders are still offering fixed-rate mortgages at high rates. If you can afford the high monthly payments, inflation and tax deductions may still make a fixed-rate mortgage a reasonable financing method, particularly if you are in a high tax bracket. Other lenders are experimenting with new types of fixed-rate mortgages, which have, for example, shorter terms or balloon payments. For example, you might be able to find a fifteen-year mortgage with a fixed rate of interest that is 1 percent or 2 percent below market rates. In this type of plan, your down payment and monthly payments are higher but your debt is fully repaid at the end of the term.

Flexible-rate mortgage

Flexible-rate mortgages have an interest rate that increases or decreases over the life of the loan based upon market conditions. Some lenders refer to flexible rates as adjustable or variable. For example, federal savings and loans offer "adjustable mortgage loans," and national banks offer "adjustable rate mortgages." Because flexible-rate loans can have different provisions, you should evaluate each one carefully.

In most flexible-rate loans, your starting rate, or "initial interest rate," will be lower than the rate offered on a standard fixed-rate mortgage. This is because your longterm risk is higher—your rate can increase with the market—so the lender offers an inducement to take this plan.

Changes in the interest rate are usually governed by a financial index. If the index rises, so may your interest rate. In some plans, if the index falls, so may your rate. Examples of these indexes are the Federal Home Loan Bank Board's national average mortgage rate and the U.S. Treasury bill rate. Generally, the more sensitive the index is to market changes, the more frequently your rate can increase or decrease.

Suppose your interest rate is tied to the Bank Board index. Your mortgage limits rate changes to one per year, although it doesn't limit the amount of the change. For example, assume your starting interest rate is 14 percent on September 1, 1982. Based on these terms, if the Bank Board index rises two percentage points by September 1, 1983, your new rate for the next year will be 16 percent.

Rate caps. To build predictability into your flexible-rate loan, some lenders include provisions for "caps" that limit the amount your interest rate may change. These provisions limit the amount of your risk.

A periodic cap limits the amount the rate can increase at any one time. For example, your mortgage could provide that even if the index increases 2 percent in one year, your rate can only go up 1 percent. An aggregate cap limits the amount the loan can increase over the entire life of the loan. This means that, for example, even if the index increases 2 percent every year, your rate cannot increase more than 5 percent over the entire loan.

Many flexible-rate mortgages offer the possibility of rates that may go down as well as up. In some loans, if the rate can only increase 5 percent, it may only decrease 5 percent. If no limit is placed on how high the rate can go, there may be a provision that also allows your rate to go down along with the index.

Because of inflation, and because they limit the lender's return, capped rates may be difficult to find.

Payment caps. Although your interest rate may increase on a flexible-rate loan, your monthly payments may not necessarily rise, or they may increase by less than that which changes in the index require. This may occur because the payments themselves are capped.

For example, assume your mortgage provides for unlimited changes in your interest rate but your loan has a $50-per-year cap on payment increases. You started with a 14 percent rate on your $50,000 mortgage and a monthly payment of $592.44. Now assume that your index increases two percentage points in the first year of your loan. Because of this, your rate increases to 16 percent, and your payments in the second year should rise to $671.80. Because of the payment cap, however, you'll only pay $642.44 per month in the second year.

But remember: a payment-capped loan doesn't mean you don't have to pay the difference. Negative amortization usually takes place with payment-capped loans to ensure that the lender eventually receives the full amount. In most payment-capped mortgages, the amount of principal paid off changes when interest rates fluctuate. Suppose you are paying $500 a month with $393 going toward interest, with your rate at 15 percent. Then your rate increases to 17 percent. This means your monthly payment should increase to $539, but because of a cap, it increases to only $525. Because this change in interest rates increases your debt, the lender may now apply a larger portion of your payment to interest. When rates get very high, even the full amount of your monthly payment ($525) won't be enough to cover the interest owed; the additional amount of interest you owe is added to the principal. This means you now owe—and eventually will pay—interest on interest.

Variations. One variation of the flexible-rate mortgage is to fix the interest rate for a period of time—three to five years, for example—with the understanding that the interest rate will then be renegotiated. Loans with periodically renegotiated rates are also called *rollover mortgages.* Such loans make monthly payments more predictable because the interest rate is fixed for a longer time.

Another variation is the pledged account buy-down mortgage with a flexible rate. This plan was recently introduced by the Federal National Mortgage Association ("Fannie Mae"), which buys mortgages from lenders and provides a major source of money for future mortgage offerings.

In this plan, a large initial payment is made to the lender at the time the loan is made. The payment can be made by the buyer, the builder, or anyone else willing to subsidize the loan. The payment is placed in an account with the lender where it earns interest. This plan helps lower your interest rate for the first year.

In one plan, it could lower your rate, for example, by 4 percent in the first year. If you borrowed $50,000 at 17 percent, for example, this would reduce your rate to 13 percent and your monthly payments to $553.10, a savings of approximately $160 monthly. Then, for the next five years, your interest rate would only increase, for example, by one point each year. After that, your mortgage becomes a flexible-rate mortgage with interest rates and payment changes every five years, based upon an index.

This plan does not include any payment or rate caps other than those in the first years. But there also can be no negative amortization, so possible increases in your total debt are limited. Because of the buy-down feature, some buyers may be able to qualify for this loan who otherwise would not be eligible for financing.

Summary. In shopping for any type of flexible-rate loan, remember to look for the following:

- the initial interest rate
- how often the rate may change

- how much the rate may change
- how often payments may change
- the mortgage term
- how often the term may change
- how much the term may change
- the index that rate, payment, or term changes are tied to
- the limits, if any, on negative amortization

Balloon mortgage

Balloon mortgages have a series of equal monthly payments and a large final payment. Although there usually is a fixed interest rate, the equal payments may be for interest only. The unpaid balance, frequently the principal or the original amount you borrowed, comes due in a short period, usually three to five years.

For example, suppose you borrow $30,000 for five years. The interest rate is 15 percent, and the monthly payments are only $375. But in this example, the payments cover interest only, and the entire principal is due at maturity—in five years. That means you'll have to make fifty-nine equal monthly payments of $375 each and a final balloon payment of $30,375. If you can't make that final payment, you'll have to refinance (if refinancing is available) or sell the property.

Some lenders guarantee refinancing when the balloon payment is due, although they do not guarantee a certain interest rate. The rate could be much higher than your current rate. Other lenders do not offer automatic refinancing. Without such a guarantee, you could be forced to start the whole business of shopping for housing money once again, as well as paying closing costs and front-end charges a second time.

A balloon note may also be offered by a private seller who is continuing to carry the mortgage he or she took out when purchasing the home. It can be used as a second mortgage where you also assume the seller's first mortgage.

Graduated payment mortgage

Graduated payment mortgages (GPM) are designed for home buyers who expect to be able to make larger monthly payments in the near future. During the early years of the loan, payments are relatively low. They are structured to rise at a set rate over a set period, say five or ten years. Then they remain constant for the duration of the loan.

Even though the payments change, the interest rate is usually fixed. So during the early years, your payments are lower than the amount dictated by the interest rate. During the later years, the difference is made up by higher payments. At the end of the loan, you will have paid off your entire debt.

One variation of the GPM is the graduated payment, flexible-rate mortgage. This loan also has graduated payments early in the loan. But, like other flexible-rate loans, it ties your interest rate to changes in an agreed-upon index. If interest rates climb quickly, greater negative amortization occurs during the period when payments are low. If rates continue to climb after that initial period, the payments will too. This variation adds increased risk for the buyer. But if interest rates decline during the life of the loan, your payments may as well.

Growing equity mortgage (Rapid payoff mortgage)

The growing equity mortgage (GEM) and the rapid payoff mortgage are among the latest plans on the market. These mortgages combine a fixed interest rate with a changing monthly payment. The interest rate is usually a few percentage points below market. Although the mortgage term may run for thirty years, the loan will frequently be paid off in less than fifteen years because payment increases are applied entirely to the principal.

Monthly payment changes are based on an agreed-upon schedule of increases or an index. For example, the plan might use the U.S. Commerce Department index that measures after-tax, per capita income, and your payments might increase at a specified portion of the change in this index, say 75 percent.

Suppose you're paying $500 per month. In this example, if the index increases by 8 percent, you will have to pay 75 percent of that, or 6 percent, additional. Your payments will increase to $530, and the additional $30 you pay will be used to reduce your principal.

With this approach, your income must be able to keep pace with the increased payments. The plan does not offer long-term tax deductions. However, it can permit you to pay off your loan and acquire equity rapidly.

Shared appreciation mortgage

In the shared appreciation mortgage (SAM), you make monthly payments at a relatively low interest rate. You also agree to share with the lender a sizable percent (usually 30 percent to 50 percent) of the appreciation in your home's value when you sell or transfer the home, or after a specified number of years.

Because of the shared appreciation feature, monthly payments in this plan are lower than in many other plans. However, you may be liable for the dollar amount of the property's appreciation even if you do not wish to sell the property. Also, if property values do not increase as anticipated, you may still be liable for an additional amount of interest.

There are many variations of this idea, called *shared equity plans*. Some are offered by lending institutions and others by individuals. For example, suppose you've found a home for $100,000 in a neighborhood where property values are rising. The local savings and loan is charging 18 percent on home mortgages; assuming you pay $20,000 down and you choose a thirty-year term, your monthly payments would be $1,205.67, or about twice what you can afford. But a friend offers to help. Your friend will pay half of each monthly payment, or $600, for five years. At the end of that time, you both assume the house will be worth at least $125,000. You can sell it, and your friend can recover his or her share of the monthly payments to date plus half of the appreciation, or $12,500, for a total of $48,500. Or you can pay your friend that same sum of money and gain increased equity in the house.

Another variation may give your partner tax advantages during the first years of the mortgage, after which the partnership is dissolved. (You can buy out your partner or find a new one.) Your partner helps make the purchase possible by putting up a sizable down payment and/or helping make the monthly payments. In return, your partner may be able to deduct a certain amount from his or her taxable income. Before proceeding with this type of plan, check with the Internal Revenue Service to determine the exact requirements.

Shared appreciation and shared equity mortgages were partly inspired by rising interest rates and partly by the notion that housing values would continue to grow over the years to come. If property values fall, these plans may not be available.

Assumable mortgage

An assumable mortgage is a mortgage that can be passed on to a new owner at the previous owner's interest rate. For example, suppose you're interested in a $75,000 home. You make a down payment of $25,000 and you still owe $50,000. The owner of the home has paid off $20,000 of a $30,000, 10 percent mortgage. You assume the present owner's mortgage, which has $10,000 outstanding. You also make additional financing arrangements for the remaining $40,000, for example, by borrowing that amount from a mortgage company at the current market rate of 16 percent. Your overall interest rate is lower than the market rate because part of the money you owe is being repaid at 10 percent.

During periods of high rates, most lending institutions are reluctant to permit assumptions, preferring to write a new mortgage at the market rate. Some buyers and sellers are still using assumable mortgages, however. This has recently resulted in many lenders calling in the loans under "due on sale" clauses. Because these clauses have increasingly been upheld in court, many mortgages are no longer assumable. Be especially careful, therefore, if you are considering a mortgage represented as "assumable." Read the contract carefully and consider having an attorney or other expert check to determine if the lender has the right to raise your rate in these mortgages.

Seller take-back

This mortgage, provided by the seller, is frequently a "second trust" and is combined with an assumed mortgage. The second trust (or "second mortgage") provides financing in addition to the first assumed mortgage, using the same mortgage as collateral. (In the event of default, the second mortgage is satisfied after the first.) Seller take-backs frequently involve payments for interest only, with the principal due at maturity.

For example, suppose you want to buy a $150,000 home. The seller owes $70,000 on a 10 percent mortgage. You assume this mortgage and make a $30,000 down payment. You still need $50,000. So the seller gives you a second mortgage, or take-back, for $50,000 for five years at 14 percent (well below the market rate) with payments of $583.33. However, your payments are for interest only, and in five years you will have to pay $50,000. The seller take-back, in other words, may have enabled you to buy the home. But it may also have left you with a sizable balloon payment that must be paid off in the near future.

Some private sellers are also offering first trusts as take-backs. In this approach, the seller finances the major portion of the loan and takes a mortgage on the property.

A new development may now enable private sellers to provide this type of financing more frequently. Previously, sellers offering take-backs were required to carry the loan to full term before obtaining their equity. However, now, if an institutional lender arranges the loan, uses

standardized forms, and meets certain other requirements, the owner take-back can be sold immediately to
"Fannie Mae." This approach enables the seller to obtain
equity promptly and avoid having to collect monthly payments.

Wraparound

Another variation on the second mortgage is the wrap-
around. Suppose you'd like to buy a $75,000 condomin-
ium and can make a $25,000 down payment, but can't
afford the payments at the current rate (18 percent) on the
remaining $50,000. The present owners have a $30,000
mortgage at 10 percent. They offer you a $50,000 wrap-
around mortgage at 14 percent. The new loan wraps
around the existing $30,000 mortgage, adding $20,000 to
it. You make all your payments to the second lender or the
seller, who then forwards payments for the first mortgage.
You'll pay the equivalent of 10 percent on the $30,000 to
the first lender, plus an additional 4 percent on this
amount to the second lender, plus 14 percent on the remaining $20,000. Your total loan costs using this approach
will be lower than if you obtained a loan for the full
amount at the current rate (for example, 18 percent).
     Wraparounds may cause problems if the original lender
or the holder of the original mortgage is not aware of the
new mortgage. Upon discovering this arrangement, some
lenders or holders may have the right to insist that the old
mortgage be paid off immediately.

Land contract

Borrowed from commercial real estate, this plan enables
you to pay below-market interest rates. The installment
land contract permits the seller to hold on to his or her
original below-market rate mortgage while "selling" the
home on an installment basis. The installment payments
are for a short term and may be for interest only. At the

end of the contract the unpaid balance, frequently the full purchase price, must still be paid.

The seller continues to hold title to the property until all payments are made. Thus you, the buyer, acquire no equity until the contract ends. If you fail to make a payment on time, you could lose a major investment.

These loans are popular because they offer lower payments than market rate loans. Land contracts are also being used to avoid the due-on-sale clause. The buyer and seller may assert to the lender who provided the original mortgage that the due-on-sale clause does not apply because the property will not be sold until the end of the contract. Therefore, the low interest rate continues. However, the lender may assert that the contract in fact represents a sale of the property. Consequently, the lender may have the right to accelerate the loan, or call it due, and raise the interest rate to current market levels.

Buy-down

A buy-down is a subsidy of the mortgage interest rate that helps you meet the payments during the first few years of the loan. Suppose a new house sells for $150,000. After a down payment of $75,000, you still need to finance $75,000. A thirty-year first mortgage is available for 17 percent, which would make your monthly payments $1,069.26, or beyond your budget. However, a buy-down is available; for the first three years, the developer will subsidize your payments, bringing down the interest rate to 14 percent. This means your payments are only $888.65, which you can afford.

There are several things to think about in buy-downs. First, consider what your payments will be after the first few years. If this is a fixed-rate loan, the payments in the above example will jump to the rate at which the loan was originally made—17 percent—and total more than $1,000. If this is a flexible-rate loan, and the index to which your rate is tied has risen since you took out the loan, your payments could go up even higher.

Second, check to see whether the subsidy is part of your contract with the lender or with the builder. If it's provided separately by the builder, the lender can still hold you liable for the full interest rate (17 percent in the above example), even if the builder backs out of the deal or goes out of business.

Finally, that $150,000 sales price may have been increased to cover the builder's interest subsidy. A comparable home may be selling around the corner for less. At the same time, competition may have encouraged the builder to offer you a genuine savings. It pays to check around.

There are also plans called consumer buy-downs. In these loans, the buyer makes a sizable down payment, and the interest rate granted is below market. In other words, in exchange for a large payment at the beginning of the loan, you may qualify for a lower rate on the amount borrowed. Frequently, this type of mortgage has a shorter term than those written at current market rates.

Rent with option to buy

In a climate of changing interest rates, some buyers and sellers are attracted to a rent-with-option arrangement. In this plan, you rent property and pay a premium for the right to purchase the property within a limited time period at a specific price. In some arrangements, you may apply part of the rental payment to the purchase price.

This approach enables you to lock in the purchase price. You can also use this method to "buy time" in the hope that interest rates will decrease. From the seller's perspective, this plan may provide the buyer time to obtain sufficient cash or acceptable financing to proceed with a purchase that may not be possible otherwise.

Zero-rate and low-rate mortgage

These mortgages are unique in that they appear to be completely or almost interest free. The buyer makes a large down payment, usually one-third of the sales price, and pays the remainder in installments over a short term.

Suppose you want to buy a $90,000 home but you find the market interest rate unacceptable. You opt to use your savings to make the down payment, say $30,000, on a zero-rate (or no-interest) mortgage. Then you pay a front-end finance charge—for example, 12 percent of the money you need to borrow, or about $8,400. You then agree to repay the principal ($60,000) in eighty-four monthly installments of $714.29. In seven years, the loan will be paid off.

In these mortgages, the sales price may be increased to reflect the loan costs. Thus, you could be exchanging lower interest costs for a higher purchase price. Partly because of this, you may be able to deduct the prepaid finance charge and a percentage (for example, 10 percent) of your payments from your taxes as if it were interest. Before going ahead with these plans, however, you or your attorney may want to check with the IRS to determine if your mortgage qualifies for this tax treatment.

Reverse annuity mortgage

If you already own your home and need to obtain cash, you might consider the reverse annuity mortgage (RAM) or "equity conversion." In this plan, you obtain a loan in the form of monthly payments over an extended period of time, using your property as collateral. When the loan comes due, you repay both the principal and interest.

A RAM is not a mortgage in the conventional sense. You can't obtain a RAM until you have paid off your original mortgage. Suppose you own your own home and you need a source of money. You could draw up a contract with a lender that enables you to borrow a given amount each month until you've reached a maximum of, for example, $10,000. At the end of the term, you must repay the loan. But remember, if you do not have the cash available to repay the loan plus interest, you will have to sell the property or take out a new loan.

Having trouble paying your mortgage?

If you are having problems making your monthly mortgage payments, you might find some helpful suggestions
in this section. But you must act immediately. If you do,
you might avoid losing your home through foreclosure.

Foreclosure is the legal means that your mortgage company may use to get ownership of your home when you
do not make your monthly mortgage payments. When
foreclosure takes place, the mortgage company becomes
the owner of your home. You must then move into other
housing for you and your family. Under those circum-
stances, you might find it less expensive to make your
mortgage payments than to rent another house.

If you have fallen behind in making your monthly house
payments or if you think you won't be able to keep up the
payments, you should follow the suggestions contained in
this section. Don't delay. Even the difference of one day
may determine whether you keep or lose your home. Do
something now! Today!

What can and should you do to save your home?

First, call your mortgage company. Call collect. If the
company won't accept a collect call, ask if they have a toll-
free number that you may call. If neither of these types of
calls is possible, call at your expense and ask to speak with
someone in the mortgage servicing department. Tell them
you want to talk about your mortgage payments—that they
are already overdue or you expect that you won't be able
to make the next payment.

If you cannot telephone your mortgage company, write
to them. Briefly explain the reason why you cannot make
your mortgage payments. Ask that a representative of the
company get in touch with you as soon as possible. In your
letter to the company, give the telephone number(s)
where you can be reached. Include the complete address
of the property on which you cannot maintain the payments. From the records you have of your mortgage, add

to your letter the number assigned to your mortgage by the company. This will help the company respond to you quickly.

When the mortgage company gets in touch with you, cooperate with them fully. Provide them with whatever information they request. This information will help them to help you. Be prepared to share with them the facts about why you can't keep up the payments and the details about your current and expected future income. Without such personal information the mortgage company may not be able to help you.

Second, call a housing counseling agency if there is one in or near your community. The U.S. Department of Housing and Urban Development (HUD) has approved over 600 such agencies and provides funds to some for the purpose of counseling homeowners who cannot keep up their payments on mortgages insured by HUD. If you do not know whether HUD has insured your mortgage, your mortgage company can tell you; however, many housing counseling agencies, including those approved by HUD, offer free housing counseling to persons with mortgages not insured by HUD.

You may obtain information about the location of housing counseling agencies from a number of sources:

1. Your mortgage company
2. Any local HUD office
3. The housing authority or housing office for your state, county, or city

Call the counseling agency and tell them you cannot keep up your monthly house payments. Ask for an appointment to discuss your problem with a housing counselor. You will find the personnel of these agencies trained and skilled in assisting persons faced with the possibility of losing their homes through foreclosure. Some of these agencies have had years of experience and have helped many home owners avoid foreclosure and save their homes.

A housing counseling agency may be able to help you

keep your home, but remember this: You must act immediately!

If your mortgage is insured by HUD and you cannot, for
any reason, obtain assistance from your mortgage company or a housing counseling agency, call the nearest
HUD office and ask to speak to a loan-servicing staff person. They may also be able to help you work out a plan
with your lender. You should also ask them about HUD's
mortgage relief programs, which include the temporary
mortgage assistance program (TMAP) and the assignment
program. These are possible ways of avoiding foreclosure
and saving your home.

If your mortgage is not insured by HUD, you must call
your mortgage company or a housing counseling agency
for assistance. HUD has authority to work only with mortgage companies that deal in HUD-insured mortgages.

If you bought your home with a Veterans Administration (VA) guaranteed loan, call the VA office nearest you.

Things to remember

1. Take immediate steps to save your home.
2. First, call or write to your mortgage company.
3. Second, call a housing counseling agency and arrange an appointment.
4. Call your HUD or VA office only after you call
   your mortgage company or a housing counseling
   agency and they cannot help you.
5. Cooperate with whatever source of help you call.
6. Usually, you don't need a lawyer's assistance.
7. Beware of people who promise to correct your
   problem for a fee. A HUD-approved mortgage
   company, a HUD-approved housing counseling
   agency, HUD, or VA will not charge you for their
   services.
8. Do something about the problem now! Today!
9. If you do nothing, and do not bring your payments
   current, you will lose your home.

Chapter 5

Maintenance, Repairs, and Home Improvements

Taking care of your home

Now that you own your home you are going to want to keep it in good condition. Routine housekeeping is one way to maintain your home and save time and money for costly redecoration.

- Washing and waxing your linoleum floors will protect them from damaging stains and scratch marks.
- Washing walls and woodwork is easier than repainting them.
- Clearing trash from the basement and attic removes a possible fire hazard.
- Proper disposal of rubbish and trash discourages rodents, insects, and other vermin.
- Regular cleaning makes your home a more attractive place to live.
- Lawn and yard care makes your neighborhood more attractive (and encourages your neighbors to do the same).
- A litter-free home and yard is easier to insure.
- A clean, well-maintained home is easier to sell.

Your home is a major investment. A little effort on your part will go a long way to protect that investment for the future.

Home maintenance

Regular maintenance of your home and the equipment in
it is a good way to avoid unexpected repairs.

- Servicing your furnace once a year can save fuel
  and add life to your heating unit. Look into a service contract with your fuel company.
- If you have a gas- or oil-fired hot-water or steam
  boiler, ask your fuel company about "bleeding" the
  radiators and boiler; this will increase the effi-
  ciency of your heating system.
- Have your cooling system or air-conditioning unit
  checked every year.
- If you have a septic tank, make sure to have it
  checked every year and cleaned every two to five
  years; this will prevent sewer back-up and over-
  flow.
- Don't forget to clean your gutters before the rain or
  snow damages the inside of your house.
- If you use your fireplace regularly, be sure to have
  it cleaned every other year to avoid the danger of a
  chimney fire.

It's also a good idea for your whole family to know . . .

- Where the main shut-off valve for your water supply is located and how to turn it off.
- Where the main shut-off valve for your gas supply
  is located and how to shut it off.
- Where the fuse box or main electrical circuit
  breaker is and how to work it.

Repairs

All houses need repairs from time to time. It should be
something you plan for when making out a budget. Making small repairs before they become big ones can save
you money in the long run.

- Fix your leaky faucet before your sink is permanently stained (and your water bills soar).
- Patch the tile around the tub before water damages the floor and the ceiling underneath.
- Replace that burned-out light bulb before you trip in the dark.
- Get a supply of extra fuses before you need one (and discover you are all out).
- Patch the crack in the wall before it becomes a large hole.
- Fix the sluggish drain before it becomes really clogged and overflows.

Some handy tools to have around the house:

hammer	handsaw
screwdrivers (Phillips and straightedge)	nails and screws
	plumber's helper (plunger)
pliers	putty knife
adjustable wrench	sandpaper, steel wool
ladder	paint brushes
shovel	oil can

How to deal with emergency repairs

1. Try to avoid the need for emergency repairs by regular maintenance and servicing of the equipment and systems in your house. It's easier (and less expensive) to make a small repair now than a major one later.
2. Find out if the item needing repair is covered by a warranty.
3. Check your home-owner's insurance policy. Some repairs may be covered under it (like water damage).
4. Keep a good credit rating. You may need a loan to do major repairs.

Home improvements

Home improvements are those major replacements and additions that usually increase the real value of your home (and may raise the property taxes). Some examples are:

- Adding on a bathroom
- Building a basement playroom
- Finishing off an attic
- Total replacement of a major system
- Adding a screened porch

Check with your town or county tax-assessors department to find out if the improvement will increase your taxes.

If you take out a home-improvement loan and expect to pay higher taxes, can you afford the higher costs?

Energy conservation

There are many ways you can conserve energy that will cost you little or nothing:

- Set your thermostat to 65° in the winter and 78° in the summer.
- Have your heating and cooling equipment serviced regularly.
- Put weather stripping and caulking around your doors and windows.
- If you don't have storm windows, install plastic sheeting on the inside of your windows to cut down on heat loss.

Insulation and storm windows are usually good investments because:

- You will save money on your energy costs.
- You increase the value of your home (without increasing your property taxes).
- You may get a lower rate of interest if you need a home-improvement loan.

- You may be eligible for a tax rebate.
- There may be special programs in your community to help pay part of the costs of energy-saving improvements.

Check your local banks and income-tax people to see what special advantages may be available in your area.

In dealing with insulation contractors and storm-window companies, you should be very careful to make sure you are getting what you pay for. It is easy to be fooled.

Choosing a contractor

If you need a contractor or repair person, how do you choose a reliable one?

- Ask friends or relatives for names of contractors who have done satisfactory work for them.
- Get names and addresses of homeowners for whom the contractor has done work and check with them.
- Find out how long the contractor has been in business (older, established firms are generally reliable).
- Get several estimates and compare (avoid a very low bid as well as a very high one).
- Check with the Better Business Bureau to see if there are any complaints against the contractor.

Beware of contractors who . . .

- Go door to door, or "just happen to be in the neighborhood."
- Quote you a price "sight unseen."
- Can't or won't give you references.
- Try to talk you into "extras."
- Won't give you a detailed written estimate.
- Want you to sign on the spot and pay by installments.

Remember, if you need a loan to pay for your improvement, and if your home becomes security for that loan (has a lien against it), you have three days to change your mind.

More on contractors

You can avoid most problems with a contractor if you:

- Select him very carefully (get his name, business name and address, phone number, when to reach him).
- Get names and addresses of references (contact them to find out if they were satisfied with the quality of work).
- Call the Better Business Bureau to find out if it has any complaints against him.
- Get estimates or proposals from two or more contractors and compare them (kind of materials, any warranties, best price—cheapest isn't always best).
- Make sure any contract contains detailed information (what work is to be done, materials to be used, warranties included, time to complete the job, total cost of job).
- Understand the contract (read the fine print; if you aren't sure what it means consult someone who can help you).
- Hold back the final payment until you are sure all of the work called for in the contract has been completed to your satisfaction.

Protecting yourself as a consumer

There are two important consumer-protection laws that you, the homeowner/consumer, should know about.

1. Truth-in-Lending. This law states that all the terms of a loan must be disclosed to you before you sign for a loan (that is, the amount you borrowed, the interest you will be paying, and the total amount you will have to repay).

2. Right of Rescission. If you need a loan (for a home improvement, for example), and that loan creates a lien on your property (that is, your house becomes security for the loan), you have three days to change your mind and cancel the contract after you sign it. Be sure to ask about the right of rescission if you have reason to believe a loan may involve placing a lien on your house.

But what do you do if:

- you chose your contractor with care,
- you read, understood and agreed to the contract,
- the loan terms were clearly explained,
- you went ahead with the improvement,

and you still run into problems?

Problems you may run into

- Your contractor took your down payment to purchase materials, and you haven't seen him since.
- The job is complete and you paid the contractor in full. One week later the work he did falls apart, and you have to pay another contractor to do it over.

Where can you go for help to get your money back?

1. Consult a lawyer or your local Legal Service office if:
   - You have tried to contact the contractor yourself, and failed.
   - The contractor refuses to give you your money back.
   - The amount of money you are trying to recover is substantial.

Be sure you get an estimate of what the lawyer will charge you. Get a lawyer who is experienced in consumer protection law.

2. Bring a suit in small claims court if:
- The amount of money you are trying to recover is a relatively small amount (usually not more than $1,000).
- You can't afford a lawyer (the court clerk can help you fill out the papers).
- You want a quick settlement (usually a case is heard within thirty days).

However, even if you win your case you may have trouble collecting the money if the contractor has left town or is broke and unable to pay.

Consider this possibility before you bring a case in small claims court.

3. Consumer protection agencies are other sources of help. There are a number of agencies available to help you in a dispute with your contractor.
- Your attorney general's office may provide assistance if there has been a violation of consumer law. Be sure to check here first.
- The Better Business Bureau, which maintains a list of good and bad contractors, can often settle disputes out of court. Your contractor may choose to settle rather than have a poor BBB rating.
- Local counseling agencies may be able to advise you where to go for the particular kind of help you need.

Remember: Consumer protection laws are designed to protect you. Don't be afraid to fight for your rights, and get help if you need it.

Chapter 6

Buying Lots from Developers

"Caveat emptor," warned the early Romans in the market-place: "let the buyer beware!" This is good advice. The Department of Housing and Urban Development's Office of Interstate Land Sales Registration (OILSR) seeks full disclosure of facts consumers need to make prudent decisions when they buy land through interstate land sales. But it's up to the consumer to determine whether or not the property is a good buy and whether or not the seller keeps his promises.

Prudent buyers seek facts before they spend money. It is especially necessary to be well informed when shopping for land for a recreation/vacation or retirement retreat. The sale of land by interstate real-estate operators is now a multibillion-dollar business. There are honest, reliable developers and happy, satisfied lot purchasers. The reverse, unfortunately, is also true.

To offer protection for the consumer against fraudulent sales operations, Congress passed the Interstate Land Sales Act in 1968. This act is administered by the Department of Housing and Urban Development. It is really a "full disclosure" law that requires sellers to register their developments with the federal government and to disclose to prospective buyers pertinent facts about the land offered for sale. HUD does not approve or pass on the merits or value of the development. It does seek to protect the consumer by assuring access to all the information needed for a sensible, unhurried land purchase. Whether or not prospective buyers use that information is solely their decision.

Lots may be marketed as sites for future retirement homes, for second-home locations, or for recreational or campsite use. The investment aspect may be stressed by sales personnel.

If you plan to purchase a lot that is offered by promotional land sales, take plenty of time before coming to a decision. Before signing a purchase agreement, a contract, or a check:

- Know your rights as a buyer.
- Know something about the developer.
- Know the facts about the development and the lot you plan to buy.
- Know what you are doing when you encounter high-pressure sales campaigns.

Here's how to make use of the protection the law provides for consumers.

Know your rights

Generally, if the company from which you plan to buy is offering 100 or more unimproved lots for sale or lease through the mails or by means of interstate commerce under a common promotional sales plan, it must be registered with the Department of Housing and Urban Development. This means that the company must file with HUD and provide prospective buyers with a property report containing detailed information about the property. Failure to do this may be a violation of the law, punishable by up to five years in prison, a $10,000 fine, or both.

The information filed by the developer and retained by HUD must contain such items as these:

- A copy of the corporate charter and financial statement.

- Information about the land, including title policy or attorney's title opinion; copies of deeds and mortgages.
- Information on local ordinances, health regulations, etc.
- Information about facilities available in the area, such as schools, hospitals, and transportation systems.
- Information about availability of utilities and water and plans for sewage disposal.
- Development plans for the property, including information on roads, streets, and recreational facilities.
- Supporting documents such as maps, plats (see Appendix A, page 119), and letters from utility companies.

The company filing this information must swear that it is correct and complete, and an appropriate fee must accompany submission.

The information is retained by HUD and is available for public inspection. Copies are available for 10 cents a page.

The property report, which is also prepared by the developer, goes to the buyer. The law requires the seller to give the report to a prospective lot purchaser prior to the time a purchase agreement is signed. Ask for it. Read and understand it before you sign anything. If you cannot obtain a copy of the property report, HUD will provide one for a $2.50 fee. When requesting a document, write HUD/ OILSR, 451 Seventh Street, S.W., Washington, D.C. 20410, and include the name of the developer, the development, and the location of the subdivision.

This is the kind of information you will find in a property report:

- Distance to nearby communities over paved or unpaved roads.
- Existence of mortgages or liens on the property.
- Whether contract payments are placed in escrow, a

> special fund set aside to insure that all payments are applied to the purchase of the property.
> - Availability and location of recreation facilities.
> - Availability of sewer and water service or septic tanks and wells.
> - Present and proposed utility services and charges.
> - The number of homes currently occupied.
> - Soil and foundation conditions that could cause problems in construction or in using septic tanks.
> - The type of title the buyer will receive and when it will be received.

Remember: HUD does not inspect the lot, prepare the property report, or verify the statements in it. HUD does require the developer to register specific information regarding the development and to set forth this information in a property report and deliver the report to a prospective buyer.

Your contract rights

If the lot you are buying is subject to the jurisdiction of the Interstate Land Sales Full Disclosure Act, the contract or purchase agreement must inform you of certain rights given to buyers by that act. This is what you should look for in the contract:

Contracts signed before June 21, 1980, should state that the buyer has a "cooling-off" period of three business days (exclusive of certain specified holidays) following the day that the contract is signed. During that period of time, the buyer may cancel the contract for any reason, by notice to the seller, and the buyer can get his or her money back.

Contracts signed on or after June 21, 1980, should state that the buyer has a "cooling-off" period of seven days (or longer if allowed by state law) following the day that the contract is signed to cancel the contract, for any reason, by notice to the seller, and get his or her money back.

Further, unless the contract states that the seller will give the buyer a warranty deed within 180 days from the day that the contract is signed, the buyer has a right to cancel the contract for up to two years from the day that the contract is signed unless the contract contains all of the following provisions:

- A clear description of the lot so that the buyer may record the contract with the proper county authority.
- The right of the buyer to a notice of any default (by the buyer) and at least twenty days after receipt of that notice to cure or remedy the default.
- A limitation on the amount of money the seller may keep as liquidated damages, of 15 percent of the principal paid by the buyer (exclusive of interest) or the seller's actual damages, whichever is greater.

Contract rights concerning property reports

It has always been the law that if the seller has an obligation to register with the Office of Interstate Land Sales registration, the seller must give the buyer a copy of the current property report before the buyer signs a contract. Otherwise, the buyer has up to two years to cancel the contract and get his or her money back. Since June 21, 1980, that fact must also be clearly set forth in all contracts.

Further, if the seller has represented that it will provide or complete roads, water, sewers, gas, electricity, or recreational facilities in its property report, in its advertising, or in its sales promotions, the seller must obligate itself to do so in the contract, clearly and unconditionally (except for acts of God or impossibility of performance).

In addition to the right to a full disclosure of information about the lot, the prospective buyer has the right to void the contract and receive a refund of his or her money if

the subdivision has failed to register with HUD or has
failed to supply a property report. While a purchaser may
have the right to void the contract with the developer
under these conditions, the purchaser may still be liable
for contract payments to a third party if that contract has
been assigned to a financing institution or some similar
entity.

If the property report contains misstatements of fact, if
there are omissions, if fraudulent sales practices are used,
or if other provisions of the law have been violated, the
purchaser also may sue to recover damages and actual
costs and expenses in court against the developer.

"Cooling-off period"

Even if you received the property report prior to the time
of your signing the contract or agreement, you have the
right to revoke the contract or agreement by notice to
the seller until midnight of the seventh day following the
signing of the contract.

A word about OILSR

The HUD unit that administers the law, examines the
developer's registration statement, and registers the land
sales operator is the Office of Interstate Land Sales Registration (OILSR). Except for disclosure purposes, this office is not concerned with zoning or land use planning
and has no control over the quality of the subdivision. It
does not dictate what land can be sold, to whom, or at
what price. It cannot act as a purchaser's attorney. But it
will help purchasers secure the rights given them by the
Interstate Land Sales Full Disclosure Act.

HUD is authorized by law to conduct investigations and
public hearings, to subpoena witnesses and secure evi-
dence, and to seek court injunctions to prevent violations
of the law. If necessary, HUD may seek criminal indict-
ments.

Exemptions from the law

The prospective buyer should be aware that not all promotional land sales operations are covered by the law. If
the land sales program is exempt, no registration is required by HUD (OILSR) and there will be no property
report. Here are the specific situations for which the statute allows exemptions without review by HUD.

Sale or lease of:

- Tracts of fewer than 100 lots that are not otherwise
  exempt.
- Lots in a subdivision where every lot is twenty
  acres or more in size.
- Lots upon which a residential, commercial, or industrial building has been erected or where a sales
  contract obligates the seller to build one within
  two years.
- Real estate by government agencies.
- Lots purchased wholesale by a person engaged in
  the building business or buying for resale to persons engaged in such business.
- Lots sold for less than $100, including closing
  costs, provided that the purchaser will not be required to purchase more than one lot.
- Certain lots that are sold only to residents of the
  state or metropolitan area in which the subdivision
  is located.
- Certain low volume sales operations (no more than
  twelve lots a year).

Lease of:

- Lots for terms not exceeding five years, providing
  the lessee is not required to renew the lease.

Sale of:

- Evidences of indebtedness secured by a mortgage
  or deed of trust—for example, the resale of a note
  generated by a land sale.

- Securities issued by a real-estate investment trust.
- Cemetery lots.

Know the developer

Knowing your rights under the law is the first step in making a sensible land purchase. To exercise those rights you also must know something about the honesty and reliability of the developer who offers the subdivision that interests you. Don't fail to ask questions. Whether you are contacted by a sales agent on the telephone or by mail, at a promotional luncheon or dinner, in a sales booth at a shopping center, or in the course of your own inspection of the subdivision, make it your business to find out all you can about the company and the property.

If you are seriously interested in buying a lot, ask if the company is registered with HUD or is entitled to an exemption. Request a copy of the property report and take the time to study it carefully and thoroughly. If you still have unanswered questions, delay any commitment until you have investigated. Discuss current prices in the area with local independent brokers. Talk to other people who have purchased lots. A local Chamber of Commerce, Better Business Bureau, or consumer protection group may have information about the seller's reputation. Inquire through county or municipal authorities about local ordinances or regulations affecting property similar to that which you plan to buy. Don't be pressured by sales agents.

Know the facts about the lot

Once you have decided on an appealing subdivision, inspect the property. Don't buy "site unseen." Check the developer's plans for the project and know what you are getting with your lot purchase. It's a good idea to make a list of the facts you will need to know. Some of the questions you should be asking—and answering—are these:

- How large will the development become? What zoning controls are specified?

- What amenities are promised—clubhouse, swimming pool, or fishing lake? Are there extra charges for using these facilities? What provision has the developer made to assure construction and maintenance? Has the developer set aside money in a special (escrow) account and committed the funds to pay for these extra items?

- What are the provisions for sewer and water service? For garbage and trash collection?

- Are all of the promised facilities and utilities in the contract?

- If funds are placed in a special account earmarked for a sewage-treatment plant or other facility, how soon will the administering authority be formed? Who will be members of the authority? When will construction start and when will the facility be in operation?

- Will there be access roads or streets to your property and how will they be surfaced? Who maintains them? How much will they cost?

- Will you have clear title to the property? What liens, reservations, or encumbrances exist?

- Will you receive a deed upon purchase or a recordable sales contract?

- What happens to your payments? Are they placed in a special escrow account to pay for the property or are they spent at once by the developer?

- If the developer defaults on the mortgage or goes bankrupt, could you lose your lot and investment to date to satisfy a claim against the development?

- What happens when the developer moves out? Is there a homeowner's association to take over community management? If so, what is expected of you as a member?

- Waterfront lots on artificial lakes present special potential problems. Is the lake completed? How many lot-buying families will use it? Who maintains the dam and pays insurance on it? How is the lake kept free of sewage and other pollution?
- Are there restrictions against using the lot as a campsite until you are ready to build?
- Are there any annual maintenance fees or special assessments required of property owners?
- Do those fees commence immediately, even though you will not build on your lot or use it for years?

This is a partial list of points to consider before you commit your money or your signature. No doubt you will add others to the list.

Know what you are doing

Interstate land sales promotions are conducted in a high-pressure atmosphere that sweeps unsophisticated buyers along. Before they are aware that they have made a commitment, these buyers may have signed a sales contract and started to make payments on a lot. They may be delighted with the selection made, but if not, it may be too late for a change of mind.

Nine dishonest sales practices

Here are some of the practices avoided by reliable sales operations. Watch for them and exercise sales resistance, if you suspect they are occurring.

1. Concealing or misrepresenting facts about current and resale value. Sales agents may present general facts about the area's population growth, industrial or residential development, and real-estate price levels as if they apply to your specific lot. You may be encouraged to believe that your piece of land represents an investment that

will increase in value as regional development occurs. A sales agent may tell you that the developer will resell the lot if you require. This promise may not be kept. Future resale is difficult or impossible in many promotional developments because much of your purchase price—sometimes as much as 40 percent—has gone for an intensive advertising campaign and commissions for sales agents. You are already paying a top price and it is unlikely that anyone else would pay you more than you are paying the developer. You may even have to sell for less than the price you paid for the lot originally.

Furthermore, when you attempt to sell your lot you are in competition with the developer, who probably holds extensive, unsold acreage in the same subdivision. In most areas real-estate brokers find it impractical to undertake the sale of lots in subdivisions and will not accept such listings.

Watch out for the "investment" pitch. It is unlikely that the lot you purchase through interstate land sales represents an investment in the view of professional land investors. Remember, the elements of value in a piece of land are its usefulness, the supply, the demand, and the buyer's ability to resell it.

The Urban Land Institute estimates that land must double in value every five years to justify holding it as an investment. In some areas the cost of holding the land, such as taxes and other assessments, can run as high as 11 percent a year.

2. Failure to honor refund promises or agreements. Some sales promotions conducted by mail or long-distance telephone include the offer of a refund if the property has been misrepresented, or if the customer inspects the land within a certain period of time and decides not to buy. But when the customers request the refund they may encounter arguments about the terms of the agreement. The company may even accuse its own agent of having made a money-back guarantee without the consent or knowledge of the developer. Sometimes the promised refund is made, but only after a long delay.

3. Misrepresentation of facts about the subdivision. Here is where the property report offers an added measure of protection. A sales agent may offer false or incomplete information relating to either a distant subdivision or one that you visit. Misrepresentations often relate to matters such as the legal title, claims against it, latent dangers such as swamps or cliffs, unusual physical features such as poor drainage, restrictions on use, or lack of necessary facilities and utilities. Read the property report carefully with an eye to omissions, generalizations, or unproved statements that may tend to mislead you. If you are concerned about overlooking something important, discuss the report and the contract with a lawyer who understands real-estate matters.

If the company advertises sales on credit terms, the Truth-in-Lending Act requires the sales contract to set forth fully all terms of financing. This information must include total cost, simple annual interest, and total finance charges.

4. Failure to develop the subdivision as planned. Many buyers rely upon the developer's contractual agreement or an oral promise to develop the subdivision in a certain way. The promised attractions that influenced your purchase—golf course, marina, swimming pool—may never materialize after you become an owner. If they are provided, it may be only after a long delay. If you are planning on immediate vacation use of the property or are working toward a specific retirement date, you may find that promised special features of the development are not available when you need them.

5. Failure to deliver deeds and/or title-insurance policies. Documents relating to the sales transaction may not be delivered as promised. Most sales in the promotional-land-development industry are made by contract for a deed to be delivered when the purchaser makes the last payment under the terms of the contract. A dishonest developer may fail to deliver the deed or deliver it only after a long delay.

6. Abusive treatment and high-pressure sales tactics.

Some sales agents drive prospective customers around a subdivision in automobiles equipped with citzen-band radios that provide a running commentary on lot sales in progress. The customer may be misled by this and other sales techniques to believe that desirable lots are selling rapidly and that a hurried choice must be made.

Hurrying the buyers into a purchase they may later regret is only one ploy of high-pressure sales agents. More offensive is abusive language used to embarrass customers who delay an immediate decision to buy. In some instances hesitant buyers have been isolated in remote or unfamiliar places where transportation is controlled by the sales agent or the agent's organization.

7. Failure to make good on sales inducements. Free vacations, gifts, savings bonds, trading stamps, and other promised inducements are used to lure people to sales presentations or to development sites. These promised treats may never materialize. Sometimes special conditions are attached to the lure or a customer is advised that gifts go only to lot purchasers. A "free vacation" may be the means of delivering the prospective buyer to a battery of high-pressure sales agents in a distant place.

8. "Bait and switch" tactics. Lots are frequently advertised at extremely low prices. When prospective buyers appear they are told that the low-priced lots are all sold and then are pressured to buy one that is much more expensive. If the cheaper lot is available, it may be located on the side of a cliff or in another inaccessible location. If accessible, it may be much too small for a building lot or have other undesirable features.

The buyers may be lured to the property with a certificate entitling them to a "free" lot. Often the certificate bears a face of $500 to $1,000. If the buyers attempt to cash it in, the amount is simply included in the regular price—often inflated—of the lot they choose.

Often this so-called "bait and switch" technique has a delayed fuse. Buyers who purchase an unseen lot for later retirement may be unpleasantly surprised when they visit the development. The lot they have paid for may be remote from other homes, shopping, and medical facilities. It may be insufficiently developed for use. When the buyers complain, sales personnel attempt to switch them to a more expensive lot, applying the money paid for the original lot to an inflated price for the new one and tacking on additional financing charges. If the unhappy purchasers lack sufficient funds to accept this alternative, they are left with an unusable, unmarketable first choice.

9. Failure to grant rights under the Interstate Land Sales Full Disclosure Act. Purchasers may not be given copies of the property report before they sign a sales contract. Some sales agents withhold this detailed statement until customers choose a specific lot. Sometimes the buyers receive the report in a mass of promotional materials and legal documents. Unaware that the report is in their possession, they fail to read and understand it before signing a sales contract.

Where to complain

If you believe you have been cheated in a transaction covered by the Interstate Land Sales Act, write to HUD/OILSR, 451 Seventh Street, S.W., Washington, D.C. 20410. Set forth specific details of your complaint and include the name of the developer, name and location of the subdivision, and copies of the contract or other document you signed. It is important to act quickly because there are specific time limits for exercising your legal rights.

Appendix A
Definitions

abstract

A short legal history of a piece of property, tracing its ownership (title) through the years. An attorney or title-insurance company reviews the abstract to make sure the title comes to a buyer free from any defects (problems).

acceleration clause

A provision in a mortgage that may require the unpaid balance of the mortgage loan to become due immediately if the regular mortgage payments are not made, or if other terms of the mortgage are not met.

agreement of sale

(See **purchase agreement.**)

amortization

A payment plan by which the borrower reduces his debt gradually through monthly payments of principal.

appreciation

An increase in the value of property.

appraisal

An evaluation of a piece of property to determine its value; that is, what it would sell for in the marketplace.

assessment

The value placed on property for purposes of taxation; may also refer to a special tax due for a special purpose, such as a sewer assessment.

assumption of mortgage

The promise by the buyer of property to be legally responsible for the payment of an existing mortgage. The purchaser's name is substituted for the original mortgagor's (borrower's) name on the mortgage note and the original mortgagor is released from the responsibility of making the mortgage payments. Usually the lender must agree to an assumption.

binder
A simple contract between a buyer and a seller that states the basic terms of an offer to purchase property. It is usually good only for a limited period of time, until a more formal purchase agreement is prepared and signed by both parties. A small deposit of earnest money is made to "bind" the offer.

broker
(See **real-estate broker.**)

certificate of title
A document prepared by a title company or an attorney stating that the seller has a clear, marketable, and insurable title to the property he is offering for sale.

closing
The final step in the sale and purchase of a property, when the title is transferred from the seller to the buyer; the buyer signs the mortgage, pays settlement costs; and any money due the seller or buyer is handed over.

closing costs
Sometimes called settlement costs— costs in addition to the price of a house, usually including mortgage origination fee, title insurance, attorney's fee, and prepayable items such as taxes and insurance payments collected in advance and held in an escrow account.

cloud of title
(See **title defect.**)

commission
Money paid to a real-estate agent or broker by the seller as payment for finding a buyer and completing a sale. Usually it is a percentage of the sales price and is spelled out in the purchase agreement.

community property
In some states, a form of ownership under which property acquired during a marriage is presumed to be owned jointly unless acquired as separate property of either spouse.

conditional commitment	A promise to insure (generally with FHA loans) payment of a definite loan amount on a particular piece of property for a buyer with satisfactory credit.
condominium	Individual ownership of an apartment in a multi-unit project or development, and a proportionate interest in the common areas outside the apartment.
contractor	A person or company who agrees to furnish materials and labor to do work for a certain price.
conventional loan	A mortgage loan that is not insured by FHA or guaranteed by VA.
cooperative	An apartment building or group of housing units owned by all the residents (generally a corporation) and run by an elected board of directors for the benefit of the residents. The resident lives in his unit but does not own it—he owns a share of stock in the corporation.
credit rating	A rating or evaluation made by a person or company (such as a credit bureau) based on one's present financial condition and past credit history.
credit report	A report usually ordered by a lender from a credit bureau to help determine a borrower's credit rating.
deed	A written document by which the ownership of property is transferred from the seller (the grantor) to the buyer (the grantee).
deed of trust	In some states, a document used instead of a mortgage. It transfers title of the property to a third party (the trustee) who holds the title until the debt or mortgage loan is paid off, at which time the title (ownership) passes to the borrower. If the borrower defaults (fails to make payments), the trustee may sell the property at a public sale to pay off the loan.

deed (quitclaim deed)   A deed that transfers only that title or right to a property that the holder of that title has at the time of the transfer. A quitclaim deed does not warrant (or guarantee) a clear title.

deed (warranty deed)   A deed that guarantees that the title to a piece of property is free from any title defects.

default   Failure to make mortgage payments on time, as agreed to in the mortgage note or deed of trust. If a payment is thirty days late, the mortgage is in default, and it may give the lender the right to start foreclosure proceedings.

delinquency   When a mortgage payment is past due.

deposit   A sum of money given to bind a sale of real estate. Also called earnest money.

depreciation   A loss or decrease in the value of a piece of property due to age, wear and tear, or unfavorable changes in the neighborhood; opposite of appreciation.

documentary stamps   In some states a tax, in the form of stamps, required on deeds and mortgages when real-estate title passes from one owner to another. The amount required differs from one state to another.

earnest money   (See **deposit.**)

easement   The right to use land owned by another. For instance, the electric company has easement rights to allow their power lines to cross another's property.

ECOA   Equal Credit Opportunity Act—a federal law that requires lenders to loan without discrimination based on race, color, religion, national origin, sex, marital status, or income from public-assistance programs.

encumbrance   Anything that limits the interest in a title to property, such as a mortgage, a lien, an easement, a deed restriction, or unpaid taxes.

equity
A buyer's initial ownership interest in a house that increases as he pays off a mortgage loan. When the mortgage is fully paid, the owner has 100 percent equity in his house.

escrow
Money or documents held by a third party until all the conditions of a contract are met.

escrow agent
The third party responsible to the buyer and seller or to the lender and borrower for holding the money or documents until the terms of a purchase agreement are met.

escrow payment
That part of a borrower's monthly payment held by the lender to pay for taxes, hazard insurance, mortgage insurance, and other items until they become due. Also known as impounds or reserves in some states.

FHA
Federal Housing Administration—a division of the U.S. Department of Housing and Urban Development (HUD). Its main activity is to insure home-mortgage loans made by private lenders.

FmHA
Farmers Home Administration—a government agency (part of the Department of Agriculture) that provides financing to farmers or other qualified buyers (usually in rural areas) who are unable to obtain loans elsewhere.

finance charge
The total of all charges one must pay in order to get a loan.

firm commitment
An agreement from a lender to make a loan to a particular borrower on a particular property. Also an FHA or private mortgage-insurance company agreement to insure a loan on a particular property for a particular borrower.

forbearance
The act of delaying legal action to foreclose on a mortgage that is overdue. Usually it is granted only when a satisfactory arrangement has been

made with the lender to make up the late payments at a future date.

foreclosure The legal process by which a lender forces payment of a loan (under a mortgage or deed of trust) by taking the property from the owner (mortgagor) and selling it to pay off the debt.

grantee That party in the deed who is the buyer.

grantor That party in the deed who is the seller.

guaranteed loan A loan guaranteed to be paid by the VA or FmHA in the event the borrower fails to do so (defaults).

guaranty A promise by one party to pay the debt of another if that other fails to do so.

hazard insurance Insurance that protects against damage caused to property by fire, windstorm, or other common hazard. Required by many lenders to be carried in an amount at least equal to the mortgage.

homeowner's insurance policy Insurance that covers the house and its contents in the case of fire, wind damage, or theft, and covers the homeowner in case someone is injured on the property and brings a suit.

HUD The U.S. Department of Housing and Urban Development.

impound (See **escrow**.)

installment The regular payment that a borrower agrees to make to a lender.

insurance binder A document stating that an individual or property is insured, even though the insurance policy has not yet been issued.

insured loan A loan insured by FHA or a private mortgage-insurance company.

interest A charge paid for borrowing money. Also a right, share, or title in property.

joint tenancy An equal, undivided ownership of property by two or more persons. Should one of the parties die, his share of the ownership would pass to the

	surviving owners (right of survivorship).
late charge	An additional fee a lender charges a borrower if his mortgage payments are not made on time.
lien	A hold or claim that someone has on the property of another, as security for a debt or charge; if a lien is not removed (if debt is not paid), the property may be sold to pay off the lien.
listing	Registering of properties for sale with one or more real-estate brokers or agents allowing the broker who actually sells the property to get the commission.
loan disclosure note	Document spelling out all the terms involved in obtaining and paying off a loan.
mortgage	A special loan for buying property.
mortgage interest subsidy	A monthly payment by the federal government to a mortgagee (lender) that reduces the amount of interest the mortgagor (homeowner) has to pay to the lender to as low as 4 percent if the homeowner falls within certain income limits.
mortgage origination fee	A charge by the lender for the work involved in the preparation and servicing of a mortgage request. Usually 1 percent of the loan amount.
mortgagee	The lender who makes a mortgage loan.
mortgagor	The person borrowing money for a mortgage loan.
option (to buy)	An agreement granting a potential buyer the right to buy a piece of property at a stated price within a stated period of time.
PITI	Principal, interest, taxes, and insurance (in FHA and VA loans paid to the bank each month).
plat (or **plot**)	A map of a piece of land showing its boundaries, length, width, and any easements.

point(s)	An amount equal to 1 percent of the principal amount of a loan. Points are a one-time charge collected by the lender at closing to increase the return on the loan. In FHA or VA loans, the borrower is not allowed to pay any points.
prepaid items	An advance payment, at the time of closing, for taxes, hazard insurance, and mortgage insurance, which is held in an escrow account by the lender.
prepayment penalty	A charge made by the lender if a mortgage loan is paid off before the due date. FHA does not permit such a penalty on its FHA-insured loans.
principal	The amount of money borrowed that must be paid back, along with interest and other finance charges.
purchase agreement	A written document in which a seller agrees to sell, and a buyer agrees to buy, a piece of property, with certain conditions and terms of the sale spelled out, such as sales price, date of closing, condition of property, etc. The agreement is secured by a deposit or down payment of earnest money.
quitclaim deed	(See **deed, quitclaim.**)
real-estate agent	An individual who can show property for sale on behalf of a seller, but who may not have a license to transact the sale and collect the sales commission.
real-estate broker	An individual who can show property for sale on behalf of a seller, and who has a valid license to sell real estate. The real-estate broker represents the seller and is paid a commission when the property is sold.
realtor	A real-estate broker or an associate holding active membership in a local real-estate board affiliated with the National Association of Realtors.
recording fees	The charge by an attorney to put on public record the details of legal documents such as a deed or mortgage.

refinancing	The process of paying off one loan with the money (proceeds) from another loan.
RESPA	Real Estate Settlement Procedures Act. A federal law that requires lenders to send to the home mortgage borrower (within three business days) an estimate of the closing (settlement) costs. RESPA also limits the amount lenders may hold in an escrow account for real-estate taxes and insurance, and requires the disclosure of settlement costs to both buyers and sellers twenty-four hours before the closing.
restrictions	A legal limitation in the deed on the use of property.
Right of Rescission	That section of the Truth-in-Lending Law that allows a consumer the right to change his or her mind and cancel a contract within three days after signing it. This right to cancel is in force if the contract would involve obtaining a loan, and the loan would place a lien on the property.
right of way	An easement on property, by which the property owner gives another person the right to pass over his land.
sales agreement	(See **purchase agreement**.)
settlement costs	(See **closing costs**.)
sole owner	Ownership of a property by a single individual.
stamps	(See **documentary stamps**.)
survey	A map or plat made by a licensed surveyor showing the measurements of a piece of land, its location, its dimensions, and the location and dimensions of any improvements on the land.
tenancy-by-the-entirety	The joint ownership of property by a husband and wife. If either one dies, his or her share of ownership goes to the survivor.
tenancy-in-common	When property is owned by two or more persons with the terms creating a joint tenancy. In the event one of the

owners dies, his share of the property would not go to the other owner automatically, but rather to his heirs.

title   The rights of ownership of a particular property, and the documents that prove that ownership (commonly a deed).

title defect   An outstanding claim or encumbrance on property that affects its marketability (whether or not it can be freely sold).

title insurance   Special insurance that usually protects lenders against loss of their interest in property due to legal defects in the title. An owner can protect his or her interest by purchasing separate coverage.

title search   An examination of public records to uncover any past or current facts regarding the ownership of a piece of property. A title search is intended to make sure the title is marketable and free from defects.

Truth-in-Lending   A federal law that provides that the terms of a loan (including all the finance charges) must be disclosed to the borrower before the loan is signed. It also contains a provision for the Right of Rescission.

VA   Veterans Administration. The VA guarantees a certain proportion of a mortgage loan made to a veteran by a private lender. Sometimes called GI loans, these usually require very low down payments and permit low repayment terms.

warranty deed   (See **deed, warranty**.)
zoning   The power of a local municipal government (city or town) to regulate the use of property within the municipality.

Appendix B

Mortgage Payment Comparisons

30-year mortgage loan amounts

RATES	$40,000	$42,000	$44,000	$46,000
12.00	411.45	432.02	452.59	473.16
12.25	419.16	440.12	461.07	482.03
12.50	426.90	448.25	469.59	490.94
12.75	434.68	456.41	478.15	499.88
13.00	442.48	464.60	486.73	508.85
13.25	450.31	472.82	495.34	517.86
13.50	458.16	481.07	503.98	526.89
13.75	466.05	489.35	512.65	535.95
14.00	473.95	497.65	521.34	545.04
14.25	481.87	505.97	530.06	554.16
14.50	489.82	514.31	538.80	563.30
14.75	497.79	522.68	547.57	572.46
15.00	505.78	531.07	556.36	581.64
15.25	513.78	539.47	565.16	590.85
15.50	521.81	547.90	573.99	600.08

$48,000	$50,000	$52,000	$54,000	$56,000
493.73	514.31	534.88	555.45	576.02
502.99	523.95	544.91	565.86	586.82
512.28	533.63	554.97	576.32	597.66
521.61	543.35	565.08	586.81	608.55
530.98	553.10	575.22	597.35	619.47
540.37	562.89	585.40	607.92	630.43
549.80	572.71	595.61	618.52	641.43
559.25	582.56	605.86	629.16	652.46
568.74	592.44	616.13	639.83	663.53
578.25	602.34	626.44	650.53	674.62
587.79	612.28	636.77	661.26	685.75
597.35	622.24	647.13	672.02	696.91
606.93	632.22	657.51	682.80	708.09
616.54	642.23	667.92	693.61	719.30
626.17	652.26	678.35	704.44	750.53

124   **Appendix**

RATES	$58,000	$60,000	$62,000	$64,000
12.00	596.60	617.17	637.74	658.31
12.25	607.78	628.74	649.70	670.65
12.50	619.01	640.35	661.70	683.05
12.75	630.28	652.02	673.75	695.48
13.00	641.60	663.72	685.84	707.97
13.25	652.95	675.46	697.98	720.50
13.50	664.34	687.25	710.16	733.06
13.75	675.77	699.07	722.37	745.67
14.00	687.23	710.92	734.62	758.32
14.25	698.72	722.81	746.91	771.00
14.50	710.24	734.73	759.22	783.72
14.75	721.80	746.69	771.57	796.46
15.00	733.38	758.67	783.96	809.24
15.25	744.99	770.68	796.36	822.05
15.50	756.62	782.71	808.80	834.89

RATES	$76,000	$78,000	$80,000	$82,000
12.00	781.75	802.32	822.89	843.46
12.25	796.40	817.36	838.32	859.28
12.50	811.12	832.46	853.81	875.15
12.75	825.89	847.62	869.35	891.09
13.00	840.71	862.84	884.96	907.08
13.25	855.59	878.10	900.62	923.13
13.50	870.51	893.42	916.33	939.24
13.75	885.49	908.79	932.09	955.39
14.00	900.50	924.20	947.90	971.59
14.25	915.56	939.66	963.75	987.84
14.50	930.66	955.15	979.64	1004.14
14.75	945.80	970.69	995.58	1020.47
15.00	960.98	986.27	1011.55	1036.84
15.25	976.19	1001.88	1027.57	1053.26
15.50	991.43	1017.52	1043.61	1069.70

$66,000	$68,000	$70,000	$72,000	$74,000
678.88	699.46	720.03	740.60	761.17
691.61	712.57	733.53	754.49	775.44
704.39	725.74	747.08	768.43	789.77
717.22	738.95	760.69	782.42	804.15
730.09	752.22	774.34	796.46	818.59
743.01	765.53	788.04	810.56	833.07
755.97	778.88	801.79	824.70	847.60
768.97	792.28	815.58	838.88	862.18
782.02	805.71	829.41	853.11	876.81
795.09	819.19	843.28	867.37	891.47
808.21	832.70	857.19	881.68	906.17
821.35	846.24	871.13	896.02	920.91
834.53	859.82	885.11	910.40	935.69
847.74	873.43	899.12	924.81	950.50
860.98	887.07	913.16	939.25	965.34

$84,000	$86,000	$88,000	$90,000	$92,000
864.03	884.61	905.18	925.75	946.32
880.23	901.19	922.15	943.11	964.06
896.50	917.84	939.19	960.53	981.88
912.82	934.56	956.29	978.02	999.76
929.21	951.33	973.46	995.58	1017.70
945.65	968.17	990.68	1013.20	1035.71
962.15	985.05	1007.96	1030.87	1053.78
978.69	1002.00	1025.30	1048.60	1071.90
995.29	1018.99	1042.69	1066.38	1090.08
1011.94	1036.03	1060.12	1084.22	1108.31
1028.63	1053.12	1077.61	1102.10	1126.59
1045.36	1070.25	1095.14	1120.03	1144.92
1062.13	1087.42	1112.71	1138.00	1163.29
1078.95	1104.63	1130.32	1156.01	1181.70
1095.79	1121.88	1147.97	1174.06	1200.16

RATES	$94,000	$96,000	$98,000	$100,000
12.00	966.90	987.47	1008.04	1028.61
12.25	985.02	1005.98	1026.94	1047.90
12.50	1003.22	1024.57	1045.91	1067.26
12.75	1021.49	1043.23	1064.96	1086.69
13.00	1039.83	1061.95	1084.08	1106.20
13.25	1058.23	1080.74	1103.26	1125.77
13.50	1076.69	1099.60	1122.50	1145.41
13.75	1095.21	1118.51	1141.81	1165.11
14.00	1113.78	1137.48	1161.17	1184.87
14.25	1132.41	1156.50	1180.59	1204.69
14.50	1151.08	1175.57	1200.07	1224.56
14.75	1169.81	1194.70	1219.59	1244.48
15.00	1188.58	1213.87	1239.15	1264.44
15.25	1207.39	1233.08	1258.77	1284.46
15.50	1226.25	1252.34	1278.43	1304.52

$102,000	$104,000	$106,000	$108,000	$110,000
1049.18	1069.76	1090.33	1110.90	1131.47
1068.85	1089.81	1110.77	1131.73	1152.69
1088.60	1109.95	1131.29	1152.64	1173.98
1108.43	1130.16	1151.89	1173.63	1195.36
1128.32	1150.45	1172.57	1194.70	1216.82
1148.29	1170.80	1193.32	1215.84	1238.35
1168.32	1191.23	1214.14	1237.04	1259.95
1188.42	1211.72	1235.02	1258.32	1281.62
1208.57	1232.27	1255.96	1279.66	1303.36
1228.78	1252.87	1276.97	1301.06	1325.16
1249.05	1273.54	1298.03	1322.52	1347.01
1269.37	1294.25	1319.14	1344.03	1368.92
1289.73	1315.02	1340.31	1365.60	1390.89
1310.15	1335.84	1361.53	1387.22	1412.90
1330.61	1356.70	1382.79	1408.88	1434.97